Smoking Out the Shadows

A novel by

Rosalind Metcalf

Smoking Out the Shadows
A Novel by
Rosalind Metcalf

ISBN-13: 978-1546680505
ISBN-10: 1546680500

Cover Design: Sanga Lynch @ Milsdesign
Editor: Gloria Palmer (movinonup57@yahoo.com)

To contact the author:
rosalind@healingstartstoday.com
www.HealingStartsToday.com

Printed in the United States of America

Dedication

I would like to dedicate

Smoking Out the Shadows

To anyone who feels like giving up

and

To those who are silently suffering.

Keep pressing forward!

"Weeping may endure for a night,
but joy comes in the morning."

Psalm 30:5b (NKJV)

Acknowledgements

I am very grateful to my children, Helena and Ramon Jr., for their unconditional love and for giving me the strength to write this book.

A very special thank you to my mother Sharon Williams, and my grandmother Mary Jackson, for pushing me past domestic life and constantly reminding me that all things are possible.

I am extremely thankful to my spiritual grandfather, Rev. Anthony Mustifa, for guiding me and speaking life into me in those moments I wanted to give up.

I would also like to thank LaToya Lipsey, Syovata Edari, Steven Hunter, Dana Chew, Yakini Shabaka (Queen Mother), Phoebe Moss, and Ramon Sloan Sr. for all sorts of help, resources, encouragement, literary, technical, and financial support, and most importantly, the excitement you showed and faith you put into me and this project.

There is a big hug and kiss attached with this thank you to my brother Sanga Lynch, for doing such a phenomenal job on all my graphic designs and for helping me to bring my vision to life. Thank you to my editor Gloria Palmer Walker for all her hard work and patience.

Last but not least, Dr. Negratti. The psychologist. The woman that assisted me in breaking my silence at the age of thirty-three. I thank you for stepping outside the text book. I thank you for not judging me. And, I thank you for seeing something inside of me worth embracing.

Foreword

Little girl loved, but lost. Little girl interrupted, but flipped the script and became a boss. Little girl matriculated into womanhood, and turned her pain into gain.

For all those who travel a similar road, in a world where cries go unheard and friends turn into foes, Rosalind magically navigates you into her world as she chronicles her trials and triumphs. Her words paint a picture that will simultaneously take you on a roller coaster of emotions that will make you smile, laugh, gasp, cry, sad, rejoice, grieve, freeze with terror, and will fill your stomach with disgust, but will leave you with hope and optimism for those beautiful souls trapped in a hidden world of fast times laced with intense misery and pain.

It all began so innocently, the love in a home with protective barriers on all sides. Slowly, as those barriers are lost and compromised, the element of evil found a way to invade the innocent mind and naïve heart of a precious soul suddenly lost within herself. Friends and helpers revealed themselves to be sheep in wolves clothing. Childhood dreams slowly curved into the worst night terrors generally reserved for the opening nightly news. Ironically, the ill twist was that all this was happening in plain sight. Imagine crying and no one hears, asking for help and no one responds, experiencing horrors and trauma that make you question your sanity and safety. How does one navigate this circle? How does one get out alive, and not just survive, but thrive?

At times, when we reach our personal nadir, it is in this dark place where we learn our true resolve and strength. Help comes in many unpredictable ways from unlikely sources. Yet, peeling that onion back means revisiting those old wounds so they can be sewn up. It hurts all over again, but the wounds do heal and the scares serve as a reminder of hard lessons that life brought to conquer and defeat us. Even more so, the scares serve as a reminder that we choose not to forget those lessons nor allow them to hold us hostage any more.

Healing is not a destination, but a continual journey. After reading these words, many will be inspired, and despite the pain some have suffered in their remembering, know that healing can begin today! Rosalind reminds us that healing begins within the individual, but may also require help from others on the outside.

A must read for all.

Ramel L. Smith, PhD

Smoking Out the Shadows

~ Prologue ~

She steps out beneath a moon-filled sky. Clouds are thrust in one direction like a vault slamming shut, concealing the stars sprinkled over the black velvet horizon. The strong breeze off the lake speeds through the city at fifty mph, nearly penetrating anything in its path. Maybe the winds are trying to stop her. It isn't the first time Mother Nature has tried to intervene. This time nothing can restrain her, so the rational, serene part of her flees the scene, refusing to watch as the other part thrashes and spirals out of control. As she fights back against the air with strands of hair whipping across her face, she sees images of black shadows swooping down, lava gushing from a spitting volcano with waves of flames cartwheeling towards her, and bodies flipping over into an endless pit—images seen before, but only in dreams.

Tugging and tugging at the wire, it snaps, each end flung opposite from the other. The mind falls back into some place, causing everything to go blank. A force fills the empty space as if it has been fighting for life to bring its rage to light. Gasoline splashes over the hood of the car. Streams race down to the pavement, striking a light and bringing the ball in her left palm to flames. She throws the deadly fire ball like a possessed baseball pitcher. Instantly, a bright-white flash lights up the area. A gust of heat and the sound of a roaring train rush through a tunnel toward her face. She turns around blindly, struggling not to lose the battle against the winds which are trying to wrestle her back into the explosion.

Driving away, she never looks back as the thick black smoke lingers in her rearview mirror. The entire car is engulfed in flames faster than gravity can snatch you down. Red whips soar from the gut like a furious great dragon, torching everything in reach. Flaming fragments fly, finding a nearby half-dead tree to conjoin in the serpent's tango, consuming limb by limb, until the entire twenty-foot tree is ablaze. Raindrops of fire roll off the limbs on to the parched, bristled hay-colored grass. Every drop finds an enthusiastic guest waiting to be entertained, and every untouched object stands by as if patiently awaiting its turn to flare up and sway with its neighbors in the winds. But the harsh sound of this raging spectacle seems to be pleading in its opposition for a libation of water to quench the thirst.

She is now standing, glowering out the window. The whisper of the air has slightly calmed down. A grayish-blue ink slowly spreads over the sky, exposing huge, sculpted clouds now barely shifting. As an automatic transmitter begins to repair the wire, the part that has fled the scene attempts to catch up. It is like a sedative begins to wear off and a hammering headache is induced.

The atrocity of what has happened starts to submerge through the friction. The second feeling is a searing pain over all her flesh at the thought that someone could have been seriously injured, including herself. Easing some distress by thinking, 'Okay, I'm positive I only burned the car. The fire had to have starved and died,' *she won't let her thoughts go further because she cannot fathom anything worse.*

It is close to three years later when she sees pictures of the damage.

~ One ~

Three Years Later . . .

Before words, it is the tapping rhythm of high heels against the uncarpeted floor that commends her attention. She looks up and sees a middle-aged woman walking down the hallway. Her presence causes an occasional stare as she moves with such grace. Black heels, khaki pants, and a white silk blouse, with an unbuttoned quarter-length black cashmere sweater, accessorized with black, white, and silver jewelry. With each step, the hair over her ears blows back. Maybe what holds her attention longer is the thought that either this middle-aged woman has stolen her clothes or they shop in the same stores. The woman stops at the receptionist desk, quickly examining the manila folder in her hand, then takes a couple more steps toward the waiting area.

"Good morning. Are you Zoe Stone?"

"Yes."

"How are you? I'm Dr. Catilina Brooks. If we can step into my office for just a few minutes, I can get some general information, and hopefully, get you scheduled for a full session."

The questions are pretty standard, the doctor confirms all the information is correct. The doctor also made it a point to voice concerns regarding her puffy, red, watery eyes.

"I would like to recommend an antidepressant."

Zoe refuses.

Then, finally, the big question with a stony face. "Do you feel as though you would harm yourself or others?"

"No."

The relief on Dr. Brooks' face couldn't have been more transparent.

"Good."

She opens her calendar and pencils Zoe in, exactly two weeks to the day.

~ Two ~

One month later, Zoe is sitting in the same waiting area, waiting to be seen. Not rising a second early, she enjoys watching Dr. Brooks approach. It is the only thing familiar to her eyes. It reminds Zoe of the moments when she felt good about herself and gives her a hint of hope for the future.

Dr. Brooks briefly reviews the notes from their last session. Documented on 12/14/2013: Client does not speak freely. Client responds to safe subjects. Client displays a great deal of emotions. Tears seem to be uncontrolled. Exhibits signs of a psychological infection. Continues to refuse medication. She slowly turns to Zoe with a soft smile, walks across the room to retrieve her, and ushers her back into the office.

Once in the office, Zoe stands for a moment, peering out the window. It is a brisk December morning. Mist laces the glass, and flurries bounce and swirl around; the blowing chilled air won't let them rest on the ground. Dr. Brooks shuffle through some papers before motioning for Zoe to sit down. As she continues to settle herself, she uses her designer glasses to pin back the fly-aways, searching for something in the side drawer. Seconds later, she pulls them down, resting them back on the bridge of her nose, then returns her attention to the top of her desk, only to flip through those same papers again. Dr. Brooks keeps this cycle going for what seems like an eternity.

Both hands on the armrest, Zoe scoots to the edge of the chair; her body language matching her thoughts.

"Did you misplace something? Or is this a bad time?"

Almost instantly, Dr. Brooks gently lays her hands flat on the papers.

"Ms. Stone," she attaches a warm smile for Zoe to relax, "I want to pick up where we left off during our last session. I asked some questions that were definitely personal, and if it's okay, I would like to revisit those topics. But this time, can you speak with more detail? Now, let's go back to your childhood."

"My childhood was wonderful. My parents and my grandparents created so many precious memories for me to look back on. Every day was a Thanksgiving dinner; you know, the whole layout, spread over the kitchen table and stove. We shopped a lot. I remember them buying us bags of clothes. It's so funny whenever I think about it because they dressed us up like little dolls. Kids use to tease me all the time saying, 'Why are you wearing church clothes?' Or, 'Are you going to prom?' And we had Christmases like you would never believe; gifts stacked up the wall, overflowing from the living room and into the dining room.

"My father worked for the city. My mother was a teacher. They both were also into real estate. I always had a very close relationship with my grandmother and still do. She's the rock of our family. She brought spirituality in the home and made sure everything operated smoothly."

Zoe's voice begins to drift off. She isn't sure why, but by the way Dr. Brooks is examining her eyes, she is positive the doctor has something else on her mind. Then she dismisses the thought with, 'Maybe I'm being paranoid.'

Calculating the remaining time, Dr. Brooks waits to see if she is finished speaking.

"I've studied your file and I've looked into your face. I hear you speak and I want you to know I believe everything you've shared with me." She pauses, taking a deep breath. "We've had an initial meeting, which was basically our introduction. It lasted for maybe twenty minutes. Two weeks ago, we had our first one-hour session and now this one. What I see in you is something so different than what I've seen in a lot of my clients who have sat in that same seat. Your spirit and faith are so strong. There's no question that you love your family and that your family worked hard to give you a comfortable life." After each sentence, Dr. Brooks glances down at her notes as if she is responding one-by-one to every statement Zoe has made and every question she's answered up to that point.

"I also would like to point out, your passion and desire to help others is a gift that could take you very far in this life. I see you as a very determined person. The problem is your background, your lifestyle, and your career choice don't add up to your actions on the night of the fire. I have no doubt you are truly remorseful. My guess is, you've fought to rise above many obstacles. Over time, you've trained yourself to mask the pain. I'm willing to bet there are some things you've never released. I'm sure you know what happens to a pipeline full of steam: It's just a matter of time before the pressure causes it to explode."

Zoe slightly cocks her head to one side and puts her left hand on her hip. Her right knee bounces as it always does when she is under major discomfort. She thinks, *'Clearly, from the moment I sat in this chair, there was a predisposition to pass judgment against me. Then she subconsciously started this meeting off with a dramatic scene because she was planning to interrogate me.'*

Dr. Brooks leans in, crosses her arms, and rests them on the desk, looking with a high-beam stare over the lens of her glasses. Her words are steady, letting Zoe know, "You had your chance to speak; now you are to listen."

"You haven't spoken a word that comes close to describing the pain and depression dwelling in your eyes. Now, I don't believe it's necessary to rip every Band-Aid off to heal; however, you cannot go through life not addressing—or, at the very least, relinquishing—the not-so-good things. I would say ninety percent of people under these circumstances, with your personality and background, would be pouring their hearts out. As a psychologist and a very-experienced person in my profession, I feel comfortable saying, not only have you spent a large part of your life stuffing painful things deep inside, but I'm sure at least one of those things was traumatizing. I'm concerned because you're still not at a place where you trust yourself to speak."

Zoe's position changes. Tensely sitting straight up in the padded chair, she gapes directly at the doctor's mouth.

Fingers interlock, her lips tighten, thin as blades, a stream of tears rolling down each cheek. Although Dr. Brooks can see Zoe is now fully guarded, it is also very clear she is hanging on to every word she speaks; that gives her the cue to keep chiseling away.

"If you were my daughter, I would tell you, 'Let's start peeling back layer by layer, until we reach the core, so you can truly heal and live the life you so badly want and deserve. This will be painful and scary, but living life full of fear is not living at all.'"

She glances up at the clock hanging on the wall, then says, "Unfortunately, we're out of time. On your way out, stop at the front desk, and the receptionist will write down the date and time for your next appointment."

~ Three ~

Zoe shows up at her next appointment ten minutes early, prepared for this session to go the way she wants it to. She's brought along pictures (more like evidence of her luxurious life) to prove to this Ms. Know-It-All doctor that she really did come from a beautiful family and treatment for the past wasn't necessary.

She says to herself, "Hopefully, she gets the point and we can focus on what matters—like my future."

Her attitude lightens as Dr. Brooks eagerly engages in conversation about the special events captured in each photo. Before Zoe realizes it, she is babbling. Some of the excitement is definitely due to the memories, but part of it is her overt attempts at trying to prove a point. Then she notices Dr. Brooks is no longer participating, watching Zoe with another one of those studying looks. Her voice dwindles to a mumble, then to silence.

Dr. Brooks can see Zoe is desperately fighting to keep something hidden. It is like there is a quiet tenant in the neighborhood no one has ever seen harbored deep down inside her.

"As a counselor, I'm sure you've learned and developed unique tools that are powerful catalysts for the healing process of your clients. Are you familiar with the inner child method?" Dr. Brooks asks.

"Yes, I'm familiar with it."

"That's great. Well then, you know, even as adults, we have an inner child concealed beneath layers of maturity and sophistication. Could you tell me about your inner child?"

Biting down on her bottom lip to keep it from quivering, she weighs up how much of herself she should share.

"Look," she says soft and calmly, "I hate it and I try hard to block out my inner child. Whenever I've acknowledged it, I've found myself in some kind of trouble again. I refuse to form a softness for a weak, ill-behaved child who wants to kick and scream at the drop of a dime. I don't ever want to feel vulnerable again, nor do I want to re-experience my childhood feelings, except the good ones."

Taking a moment, she scans the floor as if the words she is looking for might be there. Then, clamping her lips in a stubborn line, Dr. Brooks clears her throat, repositioning her body in the chair, and with a firm voice, she says, "I would like to know what made you leave home so young."

Zoe, choked with emotions, says in a whisper, "Because I hated living there."

"So, you decided to just pick up and leave?"

"It wasn't totally my choice, but I did choose not to return."

"Did your parents put you out?"

"No."

"Were you kidnapped?"

"No . . . kind of . . . umm, I don't know."

"Who were you with?"

"This man."

"Do you know his name?"

"Kingston."

"Did you tell him you wanted to go home?"

"He wasn't the kind of person you could just tell what you wanted. Of course, there were times I tried to say things, but I couldn't. I didn't know what to do. Have you ever been in a situation that you didn't want to say yes but saying no wasn't an option? Anyway, there are a lot of moments I can't even remember—it's just pitch black. Then, there are other moments I can recall like they happened today."

Not wanting to push her too hard, Dr. Brooks gently says, "Listen to me, Zoe, all the memories are in there. Once you grab hold to them and let them out, the fear those memories bring will all go away." The undertone of concern in the doctor's voice is soothing.

"I have attempted many times to organize my memories while in the process of sorting my life out, but it's like they're butterflies enjoying their wings. When a hand grabs at them, they change direction and vanish out of reach."

"Okay, well, let's try this: I'll continue asking questions, and if there's something you don't remember, we'll come back to it later."

Zoe nods her head in agreement.

"Let's go back to this Kingston person. When I asked if you were kidnapped, can you tell me why you couldn't give a solid answer?"

"Because . . . I called him for help. It was just . . . it was my fault."

"For help? Why didn't you call your parents?"

"When my mother divorced my father, he, in turn, divorced my brother and me. And my mother . . . well, she was a great mother, but our relationship always seemed so complicated."

"All right, I want you to think back, and I don't care how young you were, go back to the first situation you can remember which actually supports the feeling of things being so complicated you could not call your mother when you obviously felt it was urgent to receive help. Tell me about the incident you think caused a left turn."

"The sun bounces brightly off the slightly-opened windows, allowing fresh air to circulate through the home, easily persuading the kitchen curtains to wave hello. My mother and grandmother were cleaning greens and shelling peas, then pre-cooking and packaging them in Ziploc bags to be stored in the deep freezer. My brother Jonathon, our foster-sister Rachel, foster-brother Brandon, and I were running around the house, playing as usual—sliding across the floor in our socks, playing tag. We jumped up and ran to hide from Brandon. He found me hiding beneath a bed.

"'I FOUND YOU! I FOUND YOU!' he screamed, all the while laughing. He slid under the bed, blocking me from getting out, and started tickling me. Then the tickling stopped. He put his hand over my mouth and said, 'Shhh, before they hear us.' Right at that very second, my mother yelled, 'GET FROM UNDERNEATH THE BED THIS MINUTE!' Startled, and maybe just as confused—I'd only known my mother to be soft spoken—we both stood to our feet. Her anger was bearing down upon our heads. 'Go to your room right now!" she growled at Brandon. 'Zoe, get your butt in that living room, and you'd bet' not get off the couch unless I tell you to.'

"As I parked my body on the sofa, I wasn't sure what had happened. There was no question she thought we'd done something wrong, but I just couldn't make sense of it. I figured sooner or later, my mother would come talk to me, but hours went by as I lay across the sofa. I could still hear my mother and grandmother talking but their voices started to sound far away.

"I must have drifted off because, the next time I opened my eyes, things had completely changed. The sun had gone down, and it was much warmer and stuffy; the windows and doors had been closed. I was still stretched out, my head tilted to the side, and my right arm and right leg were hanging off the couch. My limbs had yet to awaken. I lay there as my body slowly came back to life, thinking, *'I really need to use the bathroom.'*

"The chattering from the kitchen continued, and as my hearing became clearer, I recognized the voices. It was my mother, her best friend, and my cousin's wife. Rolling over to my side, I was still drowsy, but my bladder was saying 'GET UP!' Yawning, extending my arms and legs, gave my body the boost it needed to leverage myself up to head toward the bathroom. Before rising to my feet, I was snatched by the ear when I heard my name. I couldn't help lifting my head a little and looking toward the kitchen, captured by the conversation.

"I heard my mother telling those two ladies she had caught me under the bed with Brandon. My cousin's wife dove straight in.

"'GIRL! Are you serious?'

"'Un uh, you've got to be joking?'

"Then her friend chimed in before giving the last blabbermouth time to finish her sentence. 'Oh, my God, Julia! Was he touching her?'

"'As soon as I saw them, I yelled and made 'em go lie down,' my mother said.

"One by one, they continued asking questions, giving their input, and sharing their own past stories, all the while talking over each other."

~ Four ~

Her heart starts pounding, nostrils flare up, teeth clench together, and lips tighten. Anger and embarrassment shoot through her veins. Curling into a ball, she bites down on her lip, trying to fight the emotions away. Sliding both hands between her thighs, she squeezes her legs together, pressing one palm into the other, holding every muscle in her stomach to keep her urine from discharging out her body. To reach the bathroom, she would have to walk past the kitchen, but shame won't allow her feet to plant on the floor.

Unable to hold back the tears any longer, they now stream down her face. Drawing air in her lungs, slowly exhaling only when absolutely necessary, she's trying not to let any sound seep out. In the kitchen, their mouths are steady running. Due to the strong, unsettling feelings surging through her body, her senses begin fading. The transmitter for sound is no longer sensitive, fluids blur her vision, the skin loses consciousness of its bodily sensations. It is impossible to know how long she's been lying here, but the urgency to use the bathroom at some point has disappeared. Having become so mentally exhausted, she apparently passes out with no warning.

This is the first incident Zoe can recall that sent her body down a river of emotions so powerful it shut down.

Frozen in the fetal position and body quivering, she wonders why it is so cold. With each passing second, she becomes more and more aware. The house is free of noise and the sky has started to lighten up. She can't stop shivering. Continuing to reposition herself, she seeks warmth. Suddenly her eyes pop wide open. She can't believe she fell asleep and wet herself. In shock, she jumps up and eases into the bathroom, changing my wet clothes for dry ones. Then she grabs a big towel and sheet to lay over the sofa to cover up what will be her first embarrassing secret—that, for some reason, she believes is her fault.

She is around nine years old when this happens. A typical morning for her is waking to the smell of fresh coffee brewing and hearing bacon sizzling in the skillet, the delicious aroma filling the house. Then her springing forth like a jack-in-the-box, fully energetic, ready to run and play without a care in the world.

This morning is different. There is no energy and the joy has been drained from her spirit. She doesn't understand how or why, but it feels as though she has a new set of eyes and as if someone else's heart beat within her. She feels nervous. She doesn't even want to look at her mother, and she wasn't sure what to expect of her father. Quite naturally, she assumes her mother told him since she'd discussed it with her friends. The house is still motionless, then she hears footsteps. She is relieved when she sees it is her brother Jonathon. He turns on the television, flipping through the channels, finding some cartoons.

Glancing over at me, "What's wrong with you?" he asks.

"Nothing," I answer.

A few minutes later, Jonathon goes into the kitchen and comes back with two bowls of Frosted Flakes. Placing the cereal on the cocktail table, he looks at her with the look of a caregiver in his eyes. She sits on the floor next to him and they eat. His intuition tells him something is wrong, but he doesn't pry. However, her abnormal behavior has him concerned. He starts laughing and making remarks to the television as if the characters can hear him. She recognizes the invitation in his voice to join in. She manages to push out a noise that sounds like a giggle. With no delay, Jonathon begins talking and she becomes more responsive. The sun is now beaming through the curtains and they can hear the birds chirping. It's just the two of them, like it used to be, enjoying the sweetness of the morning calmly billowing over our home.

The door to the back hallway swings open, smashing the knob against the wall, before being slammed shut. Around the corner comes Rachel and Brandon, both skipping and hopping toward the living room, then plopping down on the couch. Without any warning, all her muscles tense up. They are cheerful and ready to party as usual, squirming and flopping, instantly changing the entire atmosphere.

'GET OUT OF HERE! WHY CAN'T THEY GO LIVE WITH THEIR OWN PARENTS?' she's screaming in her head. When they first moved in with them, it was so exciting. It was like a never-ending birthday party. After a while of no downtime, it became annoying. She and Jonathon rarely

got in trouble. Their home was so peaceful, but everything changed once they came.

Her mother is up and now stands in the doorway with a soft, pleasant smile. She says, “Good morning, babies. I’m going to get breakfast started.”

It isn’t long before her father is up and everyone is standing around the kitchen table making their plates. Everyone seems to be normal except her.

She spends the majority of the day with her grandmother. When she walks into her grandmother’s house, she is greeted with a long-held hug. Her grandmother places one hand on each of her cheeks, pulling her face towards hers, kissing her on the forehead. She follows her into the den, sitting down beside her. She opens the Bible and begins to read different scriptures, explaining them to her in a way she can understand. They sit for hours, having spiritual conversations over huge slices of pound cake. Their connection has always been much deeper than the title they were given due to her birth. She doesn’t fully comprehend it, but she knows there is an overwhelming force that always draws her to grandmother. She’s blessed with a gift only God can give.

When she returns home that evening, almost immediately her temples start to throb. Her mother asks if she’s feeling sick.

“My head hurts.”

She can see the concern and care in her mother eyes. She lays her hand on her face. "You don't feel hot, but let me check the medicine cabinet and see what we've got, just in case you're coming down with some kind of bug."

Returning with Children's Tylenol, a glass of orange juice, and a cool, wet face towel neatly folded, she places it across her forehead.

"I just want you to lie back and relax. Call me if you need something and I'll be back to check on you in a few."

She watches as her mother walks away, not knowing how to feel about the love she has displayed.

~ Five ~

"Isn't it crazy how one event possesses the power to change your perception in the blink of an eye?" Zoe said to Dr. Brooks.

"Late that night, I was lying there, but this time, no tears or no fears. Days after were hazy. Interferences with my recollection were more likely caused by the battle of varying thoughts. Days rolled over into weeks. Going along with everyone else's actions, I began to act like nothing had happened. It took a moment, but after lengthy observations, I'm able to follow the rules perfectly: wake up, wash your face, brush your teeth, open the blinds to fill the house with natural light, say good morning, put a smile on your face, and if you're asked how you're doing, remember to say 'good' or 'fine' no matter how I'm really feeling. Be sure to eat, laugh, and make lots of jokes because that's really the solution for everything. And don't forget to get dressed as if it's a special occasion; then no one will ever suspect there's a problem. Put one foot in front of the other, mimic those simple steps.

"Before I knew it, I'm almost behaving like my normal self. I learned to use what I like to call the adult Band-Aid, and there is no denying it's an extremely powerful method. Not only does it create an illusion that influences the mind of others, it has the same trickery effect over your own mind. Though random reminders suggested the bandage does not mend something internally, I learned to ignore it and push those unwanted feelings deep inside me. I loved my family. I had everything a kid could ask for, and I knew it was a blessing to have a precious mother and father who I adored. It wasn't like I'd been beaten or a bone was broken; it definitely was nowhere near that bad.

"I was constantly being told about how spoiled I was, which brought on a sense of guilt. I turned around and told myself to 'stop acting like a baby and to let those uncomfortable feelings go'. I'd repeat that over and over in my head when I felt myself starting to deflate. Battling all the ill thoughts that attempted to sneak into her brain, I was always contemplating discussing those emotions brewing beneath the surface with my parents. I had neither the instructions or the courage to confront them, nor the words to describe what I was feeling. Not to mention, my child-like trust had sharply started to dwindle after many internal debates, each time coming to the same conclusion.

"There was no way I could reopen my own wound! I had just started feeling relaxed again in my own skin. Most importantly, I was aware of the agitation and disturbance lingering within me, which was scary, because if their response would be as it was before, then I would've been taking a chance of possibly diminishing the connection left between my parents and me.

"A couple of years passed and things got better. Brandon and Rachel made an unbelievable amount of progress. Somewhere in the process of their transformation, my view of them changed as well. You know, time flies when your life is rotating smoothly. I can remember the feeling of the last time I felt like me, and life was smooth and easy and innocent. What makes that memory so sweet, and maybe a little more memorable, is that it fell during the summer, which is my favorite season of the year.

As a child, I always found autumn to be just as beautiful
as the summer season,
seeing leaves changing colors from green to red, orange,
and yellow, blowing from the tree branches.

Flocks of birds traveling in the form of a huge perfect V,
soaring through the sky,
racing against the storm's great eye.

All living things prepare by gathering food and taking
shelter, but some still won't survive.

Winds
move weightless things from side to side.

Some things are rooted in the earth
impossible to run or hide.

Stripped of all its beauty,
the liveliness begins to wither away.

Autumn
reflects true faith in the highest degree.

Once the long-lasting storm has passed,
the seeds,
deeply planted beneath the ground
surrounded by rich soil,
blossom through all the debris.

~ Six ~

Early one colorful summer Saturday morning, Zoe's parents get out of bed running. Her father jumps in the shower before eating. She listens to him whistling the tune from a song through the bathroom walls. Her mother makes a quick small breakfast, which is unusual, so it's clear they're rushing out the house.

When asked, they both answer, "We've got to go see a man about a dog."

Rachel and Brandon start singing with excitement. "Yay, we're-gonna-get-a-doooggg; we're-gonna-get-a-doooggg."

Jonathon interrupts their song. "We aren't about to get a dog. They say that when they don't want to tell us where they're going." Jonathon begins pouting. "Aww, man, can we please go with y'all? It's boring in this house."

Her father puts a hand on each of her brother's shoulders. "Sorry, son, you can't come with us, but I'll call your uncle to see if you can go play with your big cousin for a few hours."

They all become mute, cutting their eyes across the table at each other, allowing distance to grow between them and their father so he won't be offended by their comments. Once the coast is clear, they launch one remark after the next, begging their mother not to drop them off at Uncle Douglas' house. His wife, Aunt Betty, is a hoarder. Their vehicles and their home are full of junk stacked on top of junk, barely able to see the surface of anything. And the mess creates this fume that literally makes the kids sick. Zoe can't understand how they live in these conditions. She was told hoarding is a disease. She guesses it's harder than she thought for some people to clean up.

Their son is just as puzzling—young, but he moves so slow. He gets his height from Uncle Douglas and his bulkiness from his mother. He aimlessly walks from one point to the next, constantly giving the impression of being in a bad mood. Poor George automatically comes to mind whenever Zoe sees him.

Zoe's mother stares at them with a smile on her face as she shakes her head. Finally, she replies, "You kids should be ashamed, sitting here talking about your family like this."

They are all giggling and yelling, "MOMMA, YOU KNOW IT'S TRUE." They can see her struggling to keep from laughing too.

"'It doesn't matter if it's true, it still isn't nice, and it won't kill you to go visit your cousin for a few hours. I'm sure they'll be happy to have y'all over, and who knows, you just might have a little fun," she responds with a smile.

She winks at them, then walks toward her bedroom. "Get up from the table and get dressed," her voice echoes down the hallway.

Parked directly in front of their uncle's house, her parents begin giving them the 'you'd better be on your best behavior' speech. Before they can finish, Aunt Betty is waving from the porch. Rolling down the window, they wave back.

"Hey, Phillip! Hey, Julia! Don't worry, the kids will be fine."

"Okay, Betty; thanks again. And we'll be back before it gets too late."

Jonathon runs into the house first and the rest of them follow. George is sitting in the front room. They can barely see him through the clutter, the crown of his head shining over some boxes.

"Hey, George; what are you doing?" Jonathon asks.

"I'm putting together a puzzle," he answers, remaining in deep concentration.

They stand watching for at least five minutes before their eyes begin to wander, looking around at all the stuff spread throughout the house, wanting to take a seat but not wanting to offend by asking, "Where are we supposed to sit?" They start making silly faces at one another, and when no one says anything, they take it as approval to carry on, bursting into laughter and playing more freely. Suddenly, the disorderly home turns into a playhouse. Swiftly, they maneuver through the main floor, ducking and hiding and screaming when they spot each other.

After a while, and with a few pushes from the boys, George decides to join us. Having run themselves sweaty and in need of a break, they go sit down on the stairs in the back hall. There is a cool breeze seeping underneath the outside door. Enjoying the seat, along with the fresh air, their activities continue. Zoe and Rachel sit side-by-side playing Ms. Mary Mack. After Jonathon, Brandon, and George catch their breath, they start taking turns jumping from the top of the stairs down to the platform. Eventually, George's mother steps into the hallway, telling the boys to quiet down. Before closing the door, she hands each of them a cold juice box.

"Let's go outside," Brandon suggests, already opening the back door.

For a split second, they are all excited, but when they see raindrops, that idea is cancelled.

"Follow me. I've got some toys in the basement," George says.

Down the stairs they go; step-by-step, the pace of their movement begins to decrease. The temperature has drastically changed. The girls clench their arms across their bodies as the chilly draft sweeps over the concrete floor. There is a tingling sensation in their noses from the strong mildew odor in the air. The basement is unfinished; exposed wires hang from the ceiling decorated with spider webs. Boxes and full garbage bags of stuff and old furniture are scattered around. George leads them into the laundry room. In the corner is a pile of toys—balls, bats, cars, trucks, mittens. Their eyes light up.

"Ooooo, look at this."

"Hey, pass me that baseball."

"Can I see that yellow-and-black race car?"

"I want the beach ball."

"CATCH!" Rachel yells, throwing the ball toward Jonathon, not giving him time to put his hands up.

The ball hits him in the chest and everyone starts to laugh, including him. "It's on now!" the expression on his face says.

A few seconds go by, and boom, a clean shot straight to the side of George's face. He isn't expecting it; his shocked expression is priceless. Everyone starts running, trampling on all the items spread over the floor, trying their hardest to dodge the ball. Zoe runs through the doorway, putting her back against a wall and standing still as a mouse, praying to not be found. There are no noises; that means someone is on the prowl. The silence is nerve-racking, not knowing if she'll be the next person the hunter stumbles upon. She peeks around the corner to see if anyone is coming, and sees George quietly easing across the room in her direction. Signaling with her hands, she tells him to go back. He proceeds as if she is invisible.

When he gets closer, Zoe whispers, "Go find your own hiding spot," then tries shoving him out of her space.

Standing solidly like a statue, he doesn't budge. Placing his hands on her shoulders, pressing with force, he propels her back against the wall. Zoe's face frowns up as she wiggles her arms and body as much as she can, trying to shake his grip loose.

"Ow! That hurts. Let me go, with your stupid self."

He tilts his upper body, smashing her between his chest and the wall. Having difficulty breathing, Zoe turns her head sideways. Bending down, his lips collide with her ear.

"Stop acting like a little baby!" he demandingly growls, leaving her ear drenched in his saliva.

Crushing her shoulder and cheek together, she pushes his mouth away from her skin. "Get off me!" Zoe's voice quivers

Those are the last words she speaks on that rainy, gloomy evening. Clamping down one hand over her entire face, he uses his body weight and the fungus-infected wall to keep her on her feet. With his other hand, he roams under her clothing. She pinches together her eyelids as tight as she possibly can. The pounding of her heart disappears, Zoe's mind goes blank, and every sound, smell, and feeling fades away—suspended from time, frozen in his stare. By the loosening of his grip, her awareness begins to return, but before totally removing *his hand, he gives one last squeeze, pushing her cheeks into her teeth.*

"You'd better not tell no one." Then he finally releases her.

Zoe's eyes open slowly, relieved to see the distance between the back of him and her body. Her knees buckle and she plasters one hand on the wall to keep from crashing down, reaching the other arm across her chest, gripping the blade of her shoulder. The numbness fades as an overpowering pain spreads above her rib cage. Slightly folded forward, Zoe looks up and sees someone standing off to the side, staring back at her. Both of their faces are filled with disbelief; that person's eyes tell Zoe they say everything.

Looking up to the ceiling, she forces back the tears that so badly want to come forth. Sinking in quicksand, the longer she stands there, the harder it is to move. Somehow getting the strength to pry one foot from the floor then the other, Zoe feels the urge to run, but something prevents her from doing so. She makes it to the stairs, up and through the house, heading to the front door.

"Zoe, where are you going?" Aunt Betty asks.

Zoe turns the lock and jerks the doorknob as her aunt follows behind. In a concerned voice, she says, "Honey, I'm sure your parents will be pulling up soon."

Zoe steps out on the porch looking as far as she can see down the dark, wet road in both directions. Aunt Betty stands by her side, pleading for an answer.

"Is there something wrong? Just tell me what's bothering you," she asks in a very low voice, looking down at Zoe, waiting for a response. When she doesn't respond, Aunt Betty offers, "Would you like a snack?"

She shakes her head no.

"Well, I can't leave you standing out here. Let's go back inside and wait for them."

She holds the screen door open. Zoe hesitates, not wanting to be disrespectful, then obeys her order. However, on the opposite side of the door, she refuses to go a step further.

"If you get tired of standing, you can have a seat in that chair." She points at an empty chair then walks into the next room.

Zoe stays there, leaning against the wooden door frame, biting her nails to the meat and ripping the skin from around the cuticles. The sounds of cars driving by are enhanced by the puddles left behind from the rainstorm. Blocking out all the noises from inside the house, she listens closely at the cars splashing through the streets. Whenever she hears a car coming, she rises onto her tiptoes, looking out the small window at the top of the front door—up and down maybe twenty times. Finally, her mom and dad arrived. The car doesn't come to a complete stop before the door is slung open and Zoe shoots down the concrete stairs. Hopping into the rear seat, she slumps down, laying her head on the window sill. She doesn't get much sleep that night nor for many nights after.

~ Seven ~

Three-and-a-Half Months Later . . .

"Okay Zoe," Dr. Brooks says, "now that it has become a little easier for you to describe your experiences up to this point, can you please tell me about the thoughts, the fears, the discomfort that caused you to have such friction with your inner self?"

"In school, the teachers drilled in us the importance of another person respecting our personal space and the seriousness of someone violating our bodies. We also had guest speakers come into our classrooms, giving speeches and showing videos on safety and boundaries. They all reinforced the significance of taking precautionary measurements, and if in the event there was abuse by anyone, we were to dial 911 or tell someone we felt comfortable talking to. I remember, in one of the videos, there were actors acting out different scenarios. My classmates and I began making remarks about what we would do if someone tried to touch us or grab us.

"Those kids were too scary to fight back!

Too dumb to run,

too weak to scream,

and too afraid to tell!

Now there I was, somehow without any control, transformed into that stupid girl in the video. That was the point at which I realized there's no black and white, no script to follow. Until you find yourself in the middle of a situation, you can't begin to fully understand the complexity. What happened that evening was eating me alive, and I was uncertain about what was bothering me the most: my older cousin's actions or the fact that "someone" didn't say or do anything to stop him.

"They say time heals all wounds. Well, this wound wasn't healing. Weeks passed and it was spreading like a virus. The darkness of this experience left a spirit behind and it had latched on to me. The spell had been cast and even opened old wounds I had forgotten existed. My natural instinct was to find my way into my mother's arms and confide in her. There is no human connection more powerful, more robust, than the connection between a child and its mother, taking on life and form inside her body, providing nourishment from the clay of conception, and never stopping.

"I sat in my mother's presence day after day, inwardly battling this painful dilemma. Although I knew all these wonderful things about my mother to be a fact (she loved me, she dedicated every day to providing for me, and she was as sweet as could be), unfortunately, it wasn't enough for what I needed. Staring fixedly in my mother's face with my eyes wide open, I discovered and decoded a scar caused by fear. I knew my mother was unaware I was awake when she was having girl talk with her friends about me, nor was she aware of the embarrassing domino effect it was causing. I just couldn't shake the feeling of betrayal that resided on the surface of my heart. The fear was that she would make me the topic of another one of their gossip sessions.

"Going to my father was out of the question from the very beginning. No one goes to him about serious issues. He was an old-fashioned military man with strong beliefs in physical correction. Living his every-day life as a soldier, even with his well-groomed, charming personality, there was still no mistaking he had a dark, scary side—a side always standing at attention, waiting to discharge his weapon.

"Nightmares slowly began to come. As time went by, those images began appearing more frequently—a long, slender, faceless, shadowy figure, curving at the crease of the ceiling and the crease at the floor, closing down on me like an eagle swoops down on its prey. Unable to scream, unable to run away, I popped up in a panic a second before taking what I felt like was my last breath, feeling in the spirit that the dreams weren't only caused by the things of the past, but they meant much more, like maybe a warning of what was to come.

"I made strenuous efforts to carry on as normal, but no matter how hard I tried, I couldn't stop myself from transforming. My attention span became short; it was difficult to focus on anything. I became jittery and paranoid, quick to defend myself, even at moments when no threat was posed. I would vigorously cry over what others would measure as small things.

"My grandmother use to tell me, 'Baby, save some of your tears.' Continuing to weep with my lips poked out, I would say, 'I don't want no more tears.' With a smile on her face, unmoved by my fussiness, she'd respond, 'You may not want them, but baby, a day will come when you'll need them.' I talked about my feelings with my grandma, but I never discussed what was actually bothering me. With her wisdom and our bond, details weren't always necessary. She'd just open her Bible to the Book of Psalms and read Scriptures for deliverance and healing. Then grabbing hold of my hands, she'd pray 'til goose bumps surfaced.

"She would run a tub of warm water and mix something into it. The most delightful and uplifting fragrance overpowered any other scent in her home. We named it the rose bath—a spiritual cleansing to remove negative energy which clung on to us. I remember feeling light like a weight had been lifted off me and I had been restored like a new person. My tears dried, and those nights, I slept peacefully until the sun rose."

In a soft, low-pitched tone, Dr. Brooks carefully asks, "When was the next time you saw George?"

"A month or so later, Jonathon, Brandon, Rachel, a few kids from the neighborhood, and I were sitting outside on our patio. This was a particularly chilly day; however, we stayed out enjoying it because hibernation season was quickly approaching. The sun was beginning to set and the evening murkiness began to film the sky. Out of the house comes my mother.

"'Hi, Mrs. Julia,' our friends respectfully said.

"'Well, hello,' she replied in her soft, southern voice with a sparkle in her eyes. 'Sorry to break up the party, but it's going to be dark soon.' She started walking toward the van. 'Say your goodbyes and Jonathon make sure that back door is locked.'

"'We going with you, Momma?'

"'Yes, and y'all hurry up. I have something to take care of.'

"Jonathon checked the door; it was locked. Both hands on the steering wheel, key in the ignition, my mother was waiting for us to jump in. Five minutes into the drive, she informed us we were getting dropped off for a couple hours at Uncle Doug's house.

"Instantly becoming frantic, I screamed, 'I DON'T WANT TO GO OVER THERE. PLEASE, MOMMA! PLEASE DON'T MAKE ME GO!'

"She began to reassure me our stay wouldn't be long. Sliding off the seat, I lay on the floor of the van, kicking and letting out a loud, shrill cry, begging her to let me stay in the van or to take me back home. She told me I was just spoiled and just went on as she'd planned.

"The first chance George got, he touched me again. I could use so many sharp-edged words to sketch a portrait predominately describing George as some sort of creature. Whenever I would look back at this situation, the questions always set in: What happened to him? How did he get like this? It gave me an ounce of sympathy for him, and somehow, it prevented me from hating him. I was only a child, but I could tell he was he was struggling with something.

"Now, I know there's no certain look that identifies what kind of offenses people will commit, and I'm sure that's the last thing any parent would want to think, but he did show signs of having some struggles. And, just like many parents, they chose to ignore it, which meant, at least in one way for sure, his parents contributed to his actions. Then they left him unattended."

~ Eight ~

Physically, Zoe still appeared to be intact. Psychologically, she'd become more disassociated from everything she'd known and loved. Her mind periodically drifted away. At any moment, she would fall into a trance—during school, in the middle of a conversation, watching television—like a switch was being turned off and on. She started forgetting information she'd once retained. As a result, it was difficult to comprehend things, which interrupted her learning process. She began to struggle academically.

Shying away in the shadows was the easiest way for her to skate by. No one asked any questions nor did she voluntarily come forth with any of the problems she was experiencing. She was smart enough to know she was drowning, but not confident enough to reach out for someone's hand. How could she explain it to anyone when she didn't fully understand it herself?

An aberration manifested in Zoe's belief system. Viewing the world through a new set of lenses, small things began to speak volumes to her. She couldn't help dissecting every encounter she had, searching for answers, trying to wrap her adolescent mind around people's actions and the purpose of this thing called life. Walking into the house one afternoon, she stood in the doorway, watching her mother preparing a big meal. As she looked, she saw a beautiful woman who was raised to be respectful and polite, with strong devotion and commitment. Those were all values instilled by her mother's parents, her grandparents. She became convinced she'd mistaken her mother's ethical conduct with a nonexistent attachment.

Loving her no less and laying no fault on her for what George had done, she came to her conclusion based on how she didn't react. She couldn't shake her questions: How could she disregard my screams? How could she not hear the terror in my cries? Something was missing, almost like there was something deeply rooted. Like a mild family curse, maybe even a spirit passed from an ancestor, from generation to generation. Zoe and it became more empowered, causing a circuit shortage between the blood line, without the flesh being aware, subconsciously causing one to overlook what would have been significant if those same scenarios had involved someone else other than Zoe. This wasn't something she wanted to believe.

Taking everything into account, the disconnect was indisputable in her mind, knowing that many parents justify their actions pertaining to their children, based on a series of disrespectful episodes or misbehavior. As an adult, she began to look at every parent crazy who used those kind of excuses, because nine times out of ten, the neglect or the disconnection started long before the child was old enough to be the cause of it.

So, in Zoe's case, just like the cases of many others, what could she have done so bad to warrant this treatment by the age of eleven and younger? It couldn't have been anything other than a spiritual attack. She began to wonder if it was her dark skin, the kinkiness of her hair, the frailness of her frame, or the closeness between her and other family members.

Or maybe it was the reflection of her father that her mother saw when looking into Zoe's eyes. Rambling through the remains of her brain, seeking out knowledge to make sense of the disjointed emotions she felt from her mother, Zoe gave up, telling herself the 'why' didn't matter because this was the reality.

~ Nine ~

Tossing and turning through the night, perspiration beading over her body, she fights with herself to get some rest.

"Phillip, stop! Please! Please don't!"

This is followed by screams, then a loud thumping sound with more bumps follow. Zoe jumps out of bed but hesitates to leave the room. She can feel something awful is happening. Kneeling at the end of her dresser, she peeks down the long, narrow hallway. Jonathon is in sight, lying with half his body on the floor and his shoulders and head propped against their parents' bedroom door. The sounds of her mother and brother weeping echo through the house. Her father marches out the back door and Zoe crawls across the carpet without standing up.

She peeks out the drapes hanging over her bedroom window, watching as her father steps in his silver pickup truck and turns on the wipers to wipe off the misty overlay. As she squints her eyelids at the shine of his fog lights, she hears his tires rolling over the gravel. She watches as his taillights shrink into little red specks and disappear. Never stepping out her room, too afraid to see more, Zoe crawls back across the carpet, planting herself back at the end of the dresser. In a state of shock, wrapping her arms around her legs, chin resting between her knees, she stares toward the window.

Suspended in time, the next few hours fly by like seconds. The hazy membrane begins fading, a tint of light streaks across the vivid black sky. Creeping out her room, their home feels deserted. No movement. No sounds. Zoe finds her mother stretched out on the couch, face bruised and swollen. Meeting each other eyes, she sees her mother fighting to hold back her tears. Zoe's mind is flooded with questions, although she asks none.

Soon her mom and the children are gathered up and taken to a secret location, remaining in hiding until the judge makes his ruling. Later, Zoe learns her father had jumped on her mother and her brother overheard them. Jonathan had run into their room, trying to protect her, and her father had thrown him into the door. Had he not left marks of evidence, she wouldn't have believed he'd done this. Zoe is devastated.

To say she loves her father is an understatement. Even in the moments he didn't know she was watching, she'd studied him. She admires his intellect, his drive, his strength, his sense of humor. Their relationship, their bond, is so special. She is his daughter and he inspired her to be an individual, a leader.

What could have possessed him to do such a thing to his family? His son? The mother of his children? How could his flesh have been so weak to abuse his precious wife who couldn't have been any sweeter to him? Not to mention, nothing about her is threatening. She is substance-free and rarely uses curse words. She wouldn't hurt a fly. Standing five-foot-five, maybe one hundred thirty-five pounds, with a personality to match her fragile size, she is perky from sun up to sundown. He knows she isn't a fighter. He also knows she would never tolerate that type of mistreatment.

With no hesitation, she files for a divorce. Zoe's father is furious. The court issues a restraining order against her father due to his violent behavior. Through all that's going on, her mother has yet to part her lips with any negativity toward him. It is clear to the children she still loves him, but now she fears him. Really there is no need to say anything good or bad; everyone's actions speak loud and clear.

In one night, their world is flipped upside down with no warning. The thought has never crossed their minds that something like this could happen. They had just had family game night and ate Rocky Rococo's pizza the night before he snapped. There were no preconceived opinions about choosing between their parents. A sudden choice no child should have to make is thrust upon them. Their mother encourages them to maintain contact with their father, but rage has taken control of him. The man his kids knew was no longer present. Prompted by natural instincts, they gravitate toward their mother. Once the judge starts dividing their assets, he acts like everyone is his enemy. Papers are delivered to their home.

'What?! He's fighting for custody? So, my father does want me?' Zoe thinks.

Zoe pauses. It feels like her heart is thawing. For the first time in a while, she has a warm, tingly sensation inside her body and she smiles. Then, guilt snuggles around every bone that holds her together. Although she would never leave her mother, she still wants her father in her life. Now, she's beating herself up with her own thoughts. She feels horrible for judging him, for assuming the worst, for not leaving room for error. She feels she should have known he would never leave her. How could she let his sudden departure overshadow the committed man he's proven to be?

Zoe and Jonathon go visit him a few times. Things are nowhere near the same, but she is grateful for every minute they spend together, figuring once everything gets settled, they'll have a somewhat normal relationship again. Finally, the court battles come to an end. There are ordered to split in half all the assets they've accumulated over the last seventeen years—including the kids. Knowing the divorce is finalized causes a bittersweet feeling. It shines a light on the fact their family is permanently broken. However, the anticipation of moving forward brings a small amount of relief. However, instead of them growing closer, it seems like their father starts pulling away.

Trying not to make any assumptions like before, uncomplainingly, Zoe continues reaching out, patiently waiting for him to choose to be her father again. The one-way relationship becomes too painful. She comes to the realization she is seeking love from a man who somehow has become satisfied with only having been her producer. She thinks back over the countless times she's sat on the right side of her father with a pile of pecans in front of them. He could crack 'em straight down the middle with one squeeze and neither side of the nut would crumble. As fast as he cracked and opened ’em, was as fast as she ate ’em.

The entire time he was emptying out everything, he knew everything he’d done, everything he'd seen, and everything he’d thought. His stories were always so detailed and adventurous, speaking in riddles, that Zoe clung to every word. He’d talk about the old days, cars, other countries, people she’d never seen in her life. Some of the stories she’d heard before, which sometimes made it easy to tell where the embroidery began and the truth ended. She’d sit there, enjoying listening to his deep, distinctive sound, seeing the enthusiasm in his movements.

Suddenly, the sound of his voice she’d loved so much begins to sound like nails on a chalkboard. He makes walking away from her and her brother look so simple. She can’t hold on any longer. She has to let go, but every night, she prays her father will miss her and show up at their front door. Seasons pass, then birthdays, and holidays. She suppresses her emotions and pretends he is no longer living.

One morning Zoe’s mother and grandmother are sitting in the kitchen, talking over cups of coffee. She sits at the table, listening as they discuss life in the south and how things have changed. Zoe’s grandmother starts reminiscing about her husband and their many business ventures, how they worked together as a team, and were determined to provide a good life for their children. She goes into detail about the first car they purchased for their daughter Julia and a list of other special moments. It seems as if those many topics trigger some hurtful memories as well.

To Zoe's surprise, her mother becomes very vocal about her own father, stating facts which she believes support her argument that he treated her differently. Zoe's grandmother doesn't disagree; she just continues talking from a joyful point of view, reminding Julia of the love he showed all his children.

Zoe leaves the table with a more-sympathetic attitude, knowing that forty years has passed and she can still hear in her mother's voice the unresolved pain. Although it is the same pain being inflicted upon her, her soul saddens because she understands the impact of those familiar feelings. She's developed more sensitivity to other people's emotional states and how it affects their actions. At the same time, Zoe receives some sort of enlightenment from listening to their conversation, filling a portion of her heart with relief.

Zoe thinks, *'Okay, maybe there's nothing wrong with me. I was searching for a logical reason, when all along maybe my mother is only imitating a cycle possibly caused by her father.'*

She is thankful for that information. It brings some calmness to her mind, but unfortunately, by this time, her spirit is already shattered. Loneliness covers her like an iron blanket, making her feel like she doesn't belong anywhere, and she is most uncomfortable in her own home—thirteen years old, just graduated from the eighth grade, struggling in every area of her life.

How does a child properly navigate in a coded system where everyone is doing the total opposite of what is vocally presented? Difficult is an understatement to describe the challenge of getting close to her. The pain turns into resentment. She doesn't trust anyone. Sabotaging relationships is less stressful than being surrounded by people who will eventually transform into something unknown. If you were not in her heart prior to this point, there is no way to enter.

Mentally, Zoe shuts everyone out except her grandmother, her cousin Savannah, and god-sister Maria. These are the ones she feels at ease around; mainly because neither of them triggers any bad memories. Without realizing it, they each give her a little hope in their own different ways. Savannah and Zoe are the same age, Maria a few years older than them. Bonded together like blood sisters, they begin to explore the city—basketball games, football games, carnivals, the malls, concerts. Their adventurous personalities make it easier for Zoe to elude thoughts while in their presence.

With Savannah, there is no time to think about the past or the future. It is all about the present moment and there is never a dull second. If they sit down to watch a movie, five minutes into it, she's jumping up to her feet, unable to contain herself, whining in her Valley girl voice, "Like, oh my God, I'm so bored." Savannah's vibrant spirit is what makes her so special. She has a bronze tint to her skin and thick sandy-brown, tumbleweed hair. Her style of clothing articulates her inner spunk—lots of bright colors, usually something flowy. Wherever she appears, it's like opening the curtains on a dark room—radiant and full of life!

Maria projects a welcoming vibe due to her many talents—athletic, singer, dancer, humorous—an all-around entertainer which is complimented by her height, curves, and a caramel complexion. Maria is much-more-complicated than Savannah. What you see isn't always what you get. If she wants something, she goes after it. Sometimes she doesn't even really want it; she just gets some crazy thrill out of playing games, which is right up Zoe's alley.

In so many ways, they give each other a healthy balance. They have a spiritual connection which adds depth to their relationship. They speak their own language and understand one another when no one else can. It is the summer of 1995, blazing hot, people everywhere. The fire hydrants stay open. Water balloons are being thrown. Basketball courts are crowded from early morning to nightfall. Double-Dutch ropes clack on every block. Children walk back and forth to the penny-candy store.

No matter what Zoe does and how sunny the day is, a stormy cloud stays overhead. Smiling through the rain, through the migraines, Zoe forces herself to keep going because it's so important to look normal, hoping to awaken one day and the sickening feeling that has become natural is gone.

They spend a lot of nights babysitting at Carrie's house, Maria's older sister. Carrie is in her mid-twenties and she's a pretty cool big sister. She drives them to the mall and takes them to special events. Sometimes, she lets Maria use her car for an hour or so. In return, they watch her children when she goes out at night. Carrie's friends turn into her enemies. Initially, Zoe assumes they're all jealous of Carrie because she has a thin build and is very girly, smart, and mellow. She knows Carrie isn't the type to initiate a fight, which makes the issues she is having with these girls she was once close to even more bizarre. Carrie talks openly about the threatening and confrontational gestures made toward her, but she doesn't discuss where it actually stemmed from. Zoe is never one to ask a lot of questions, probably because her mind stays filled with her own problems.

Late one evening, when Carrie returns home, she is outraged and extremely emotional. She asks them to go with her by Charlie's house, the father of her youngest child. People tolerate him, but nobody really cares for him. This stumpy guy is a real-life slime ball. Mid-twenties and disrespectful, maybe his demeanor is to compensate for his lack of height. Even when he smiles, anyone can see he isn't to be trusted, but by the urgency in Carrie's voice, they feel obligated to follow. The gut feeling of this being a bad idea causes Zoe to stagger behind.

It seems as if Charlie is waiting and ready; he greets them at the corner before they reach his house. He and Carrie instantly begin yelling. With no warning, Charlie's fist is swinging through the air. Carrie curls up, trying to protect her face. The young girls are screaming, begging him to stop. Maria runs closer to grab her sister. Charlie rises with pride, like the slime ball he is, punching Maria square in the face as if she is a grown man, when in reality, she's a teenage girl who's never laid a hand on him and she's the auntie of his newborn child. Blood squirts copiously from her nose.

A little time passes and Carrie is back in his arms. Everyone is shocked with disbelief. The people who once were biting their tongues, now, out of anger, are laying their thoughts out on the table. The story behind the drama is no longer a mystery. Charlie is in a relationship with another woman. They have been together for years and they too share a child. He is having an affair with Carrie and now it's all out in the open. The worst part is Carrie is supposed to be his woman's best friend. Zoe quickly understands now why her friends despise her. No one loves her any less and everyone supports her as much as possible.

When Charlie gets around to it, he apologizes to Maria. No one totally forgives him, but the reality is, no matter what anyone does or says, Carrie is going to continue dealing with him. The easiest solution is to accept it and move on. His cockiness proves he isn't sincerely remorseful. In fact, her acceptance of his behavior feeds his devilish spirit, spawning him into something worse than what he was before. His presence puts a sparkle in Carrie's eyes, but Charlie is more aroused by the suppressed discomfort he sees in the faces of his victim's loved ones.

Disregarding all boundaries, Charlie dedicates a large portion of his days to mischievously parading around, making sure everybody catches more than just a glimpse of his show. Slowly driving up and down the block, he blows the horn of his car every time he passes them, even more so when Carrie isn't present. He goes out of his way to speak to Zoe and Maria, following it up with a creepy compliment. It isn't what he says, it's how he chooses to say it—the tone of his voice, the little freakish giggle before and after his remarks, the one-too-many steps he takes toward her, saying, "Man, Zoe, that sure is a nice outfit you got on", causing her to take a step or two backward. Based on the facial expressions when he comes around and the sighs of relief trailing his departure, Zoe is positive she isn't the only one receiving these additional eerie vibes from Charlie.

Since no one else brings up the conversations, Zoe keeps silent as well—until Maria makes a comment, and with no delay, Zoe chimes right in. They are standing outside Maria's house. Summer is winding down. The sun still shines brightly and there's a mild breeze whipping by. They both have on their team starter sweatshirts, going to a basketball game held at a nearby high school. Maria's is Duke and Zoe's is Miami. They're wearing matching tennis skirts and both have their hair pulled into one big curly ponytail. With time to spare, they hang out in front of the house, enjoying the day and running their mouths.

Here Charlie comes, walking down the street, drifting from one side of the sidewalk to the other like he's under the influence of something. Words begin to fade away the closer he gets, and the closer he comes, the more his face lights up.

"Hey; how's it going?" he asks with a big smile.

"Hey, Charlie," they both mumble.

As he passes, they give each other the crazy eye, trying to restart their conversation from where they left off. Maria seems slightly distracted. A minute later, as if she can't hold it in any longer, she impulsively blurts out, "Ugh! Dude makes me so uncomfortable."

Zoe is thinking the same thing, so there's no need to ask who she's referring to. Sighing with relief, "Yeah; me, too," Zoe responds, as if a weight is being lifted off her shoulders.

Maria's eyelids slowly lower, her gaze dropping to the ground. Embarrassment is trapped on her face as she says, "He makes me feel weird and he makes comments about my breasts being big."

Zoe's brows raise as she pauses for a few seconds, staring at Maria and thinking, *'What a jerk!'* After taking a deep breath, she replies, "Yeah, he makes me feel very uncomfortable too."

The reluctance to carry this discussion further floats between the two of them. Although they've done nothing wrong, maybe it is the love for Carrie causing their hesitation to continue this conversation. More than likely, a large portion of their silence stems from the same reason that makes Charlie more confident in acting like an animal: Carrie's willingness to maintain a relationship with him.

Minutes pass by, then a new topic comes about. Before long, they're at the basketball game. Neither of them revisit that conversation; it's like it never happened.

~ Ten ~

"When I was younger, I use to fantasize about being a teenager in high school, picturing myself in great shape, and because I've always had long legs, I figured I'd be tall. I visualized myself running at lightning speed around the track field and the crowd cheering as the announcer called my name for a trophy. Performing at the top of my class, I would be confident I would achieve everything I set out to do. Outside of school, I would always be busy doing photo shoots, preparing for my huge modeling career. I saw a beautiful, self-assured, free-spirited person.

What happened?

Something happened . . . and why did it happen?

This life is the complete opposite of what I'd imagined!"

These are the thoughts racing through Zoe's head as she sits at the desk farthest from her teacher and peers. The desire to participate in any activities is gone. The only thing she is sure of is that she is crumbling at a rapid pace. Her visions have vanished and there is no sight past her misery.

Most people she encounters compliment her appearance, constantly telling her, "You are so gorgeous", "You have the prettiest smile". She spends a lot of time looking in the mirror, studying the image reflected back at her, wanting to see what they see. Turning her face, she views it from different angles, smiling, frowning, making all kinds of facial expressions. Sometimes bursting into laughter, and other times, she begins sobbing. Staring into reflective surfaces is both fascinating and terrifying—searching for the person she lost, and trying to make a connection with the girl in her head, the one in her heart, and the one people perceived her to be. Maybe her image compromises their capacity to see deeper than the surface.

On special occasions, but only for a split second, Zoe can see the face that others perpetually point out. She mostly sees a mystery, something with the ability to transform easily, which definitely isn't the person she feels herself to be—as if the mirror has cast a stranger back and they are carefully examining each other. Her spirit and mind begin to evaporate. In desperate need of a comforter, of understanding, she hears a voice telling her to turn to God. By now, she knows no human can help her. She starts praying all the time, like a person diagnosed with a deadly disease. She sometimes attends church. Feeling as though she should be there every time the doors are open, she now makes sure not to leave a long gap between visits.

Maria and Zoe continue babysitting for Carrie. Her relationship with Charlie is an on-again/off-again ordeal, so Carrie starts dating other guys. She is always going out somewhere, which is fine with the girls. They want to see her smiling, even though she does a great job trying to conceal the pain. Charlie bulldozes at least once a month into her life. That her heart is still wounded is obvious, and as her loved ones, they cheer Carrie on to find happiness.

~ Eleven ~

Winter has come and is finally winding down, leaving just enough snow to barely cover the grass. One Friday, after school, they meet up at Carrie's house to babysit as planned, only to find out her engagement has been canceled. Carrie decides to cook dinner. The girls hang around, talking and playing with the kids. It could be the nice weather beginning to ease around the city, or perhaps people are bored and looking for something to do, but suddenly, the phone won't stop ringing; following the calls are knocks at the front door. The quiet evening turns into a mini-party.

Even Brittany comes by, which is a pleasant surprise. Brittany is a junior in high school and working full time as a hair dresser, so they usually don't see her unless one of them is getting their hair done. With her talent, she attracts a large clientele base, larger than most beauticians with a cosmetology license.

Zoe is usually the youngest one around, yet she is the one people feel most comfortable sharing their secrets with. Maybe they think she's dumb and naive, or maybe they can see how well she does holding her own secrets, which makes them feel like they can trust her to hold theirs too. The truth is, her rude introduction to the harsh reality of this world has caused so much internal mayhem, she has no interest in anyone else's personal life, especially if it has nothing to do with her.

A few hours go by and Brittany walks up. "I gotta make a quick run. Come ride with me."

Zoe's mood starts to shift. The sound of getting away from the crowd and getting some fresh air is music to her ears. Without giving it a second thought, "Okay," she replies. Grabbing her coat, she heads behind Brittany out the door. About ten minutes into the drive, Brittany starts to give Zoe a little more information.

"My friend asked me to meet him for a few minutes at this restaurant on the east side of town."

"You finna sit down and eat?" Zoe asks.

"Nah; he said he just wanna see me."

'Okay,' Zoe thinks as Brittany forces her vehicle into a tight parking spot.

When they walk through the doors of the restaurant, charging toward them is an older guy in preppy attire, smiling from ear to ear, whose eyes light up like a kid on Christmas morning.

"Brittany, it's so good to see you. I thought you weren't coming. You look wonderful." Pulling her hand, he invites her in for a hug.

Kindly resisting and glancing over to her side, she says, "This is my little cousin Zoe and this is Carl."

"Oh, I'm sorry; I didn't notice you standing there," he apologizes, initiating a handshake. "It's nice to meet you, Zoe. Let's go find a seat."

Unable to contain his excitement, he bounces as he walks, talking non-stop. He seems to be a very friendly person, but his giddiness makes them suspicious.

'Is it Brittany's presence that has this guy on cloud nine, or is he high or drunk?'

The place isn't a traditional restaurant. Arcade games line the walls and there's a line of huge pool tables with a more-private dining area in the back. There's a diverse crowd of all ages. Zoe doesn't feel like there's any danger, but something keeps her on the edge of her seat. Tuning out their conversation, Zoe scans the scenery. Soon a waitress comes by, asking to take their orders.

"Would y'all like anything?" Carl offers.

No one is hungry so they all order sodas. When the young lady returns with their drinks, Carl excuses himself and Brittany from the table. Zoe is happy they've decided to walk around. Scooting back in the chair, her nerves start to relax as she hopes they stay away until time to walk out the door. Her center seat gives a clear view of the establishment. Entertained by her thoughts and by watching the other guests enjoy themselves, she doesn't notice when someone approaches the table.

Assuming her reaction shows just how startled she is by the unexpected company, his first words are, "Pardon me; I didn't mean to scare you." Helping himself to a seat, without taking a break between sentences, he says, "I'm here with Carl. I was on a call when y'all came in. What's your name?"

"Zoe."

"All right, Ms. Zoe; well, I'm Kingston." His beady black eyes seem to pierce the side of her head.

"Um, I think your friend walked over there." She points in the direction they walked off in for him to go find Carl.

"Yeah? Well, I wanna sit here and wait for him to come back, if that's okay with you?"

He isn't really asking for her permission, just adding the question mark at the end of his statement to soften his tone. A few minutes go by with nothing being said.

"Are you uncomfortable?" he inquires.

'Totally,' she thinks, but says, "No, I'm fine."

"It seems like something's bothering you."

Zoe smiles to prove she isn't in a bad mood.

"You should smile all the time. You're so beautiful, you just made the whole room sparkle."

She thanks him for the nice words, even though it makes a wheel turn in her head. *'Was that a compliment or was he flirting with me?'* Almost every day she is around older men in her community, some in passing, but mainly because most people she associates with are older than her. Here and there, she's noticed a few men possibly looking at her longer than they probably should or giving more compliments than needed. But older men being attracted to her has never crossed her mind. She is always introduced as the little sister or little cousin, and she is used to being treated as such.

By the looks of it, this guy could easily be about fifteen years older than Zoe—her body and face are as a girl in her early teens, and she is less-developed than the majority of her peers; hardly any tissue has formed surrounding her chest area; five-foot-four, one hundred ten pounds, skin and bones; ponytail on the crown of her head, jeans, and high-top Nikes—so she brushes off the probability of this old man being flirtatious.

"What grade are you in?"

"Ninth."

"Man, I remember my freshman year. It's crazy how time flies."

He pauses. It seems like visions from his younger days came to mind. Then the questions continue. "So, what, you're about fifteen, huh?"

"Fourteen."

"What's your favorite subject? How many siblings do you have? Are you the baby?"

As the questions keep coming, her responses get dryer, which lead to Kingston sounding a little snappy.

"What, you don't like talking or something?"

Feeling under pressure to confess, she responds, "Not all the time, I don't."

He stares at her kind of like he's shocked; then he says, "You know it's kind of crazy. I can't really explain it, but when I look into your eyes, I feel like they're telling me a story. I would love to get to know more about you. Maybe we can be friends."

The thought flies straight from her brain out her mouth. "Why would you want to be my friend?"

Standing to his feet and stepping directly in front of Zoe, mashing one hand on the table to remain balanced while leaning into her face, he says, "There's no pressure. I just want us to stay in contact—in case you ever need someone to call on. You never know what could happen. Everybody needs somebody."

His choice of words is so simple, yet something has her confused. If those exact words had come from the lips of anyone else, maybe it would have been considered a standard conversation. For some reason, his presence seems ridiculously strong, almost yelling friction. This makes no sense. He is pleased by the fact she doesn't know how to respond to him. Instead of backing down, he swells up, becoming more empowered by her weakness.

Holding his cell phone in the palm of his hand, he says, “Give me your number. We can finish talking later.”

“I can’t.”

“You don’t have a number you can give me?”

Regardless of what he says, she knows the choice is ultimately hers whether to give him a number. But in some weird way, in the heat of the moment, she feels a little pressured. She gives him the number to Nicole’s house, and in return, he gives her space between their bodies.

“I’ll be getting in touch with you soon.”

Relieved to see Brittany and Carl walking toward them, she waves her hand, signaling to head for the door.

That weekend, Kingston calls repeatedly. Zoe tells everyone to tell him she isn’t there. His persistence pours over into the weekdays. Nicole calls Zoe at her mother’s house wanting to know who is the man who keeps calling her house. The little information she has, she doesn’t share, only saying, “When his number comes up on the caller ID, just don’t answer it. He’ll stop calling.”

The next Saturday, the girls meet each at Carrie's house. As they’re watching television, the phone rings. Zoe's natural reaction is to grab the receiver.

“Hello.”

“Hi; may I speak with Zoe?”

Knowing by the voice the person on the other end of the line was Kingston, she is reluctant to identify herself, so she says, “Who is this?”

He responds, “Kingston; is this Zoe?”

‘Why did I say yes when I could’ve said no?’ she thinks as he swiftly crams a lot of words together like he doesn’t have a second to spare for breathing.

This call consists of him flooding her with his personal information, organized perfectly, highlighting what he feels to be his best features.

“I am the owner of Endless Communications. I sell Motorola devices—cellphones, pagers, walkie talkies. Everybody in this city shops with me. I’m making so much money, that soon I’ll be opening up locations nationwide.” He goes on, saying, “I moved here from lower Michigan. I’ve got a place out in the suburbs right outside the city.”

He struggles to sound like a businessman by talking so fast, but he can’t keep the street slang hidden. At some point, Zoe’s immaturity kicks in and she begins to snicker. For a while, she was trying to hold it in because he doesn’t come off as a person with a sense of humor. She can’t have been more correct.

“Can I ask you what’s so funny?”

The gravity of his tone reminds Zoe of her father. She responds like a child unable to speak its mind. “Nothing; nothing’s funny.”

The truth is she doesn’t comprehend the purpose of his saying all those things. The way he talks sounds so foreign, actually kind of animated. It’s one of those situations, when something is just so crazy, you can’t help giggling.

“Check this out: I really don’t care to talk on the phone. I’ve got some business I need to discuss with you in person.” Frustration is in his voice. “What’s the address where you are?”

“I can’t give you my address.”

“You think I don’t know you don’t live there? Come on, man. That’s your sister or your cousin’s house. It’s not like I’m going to park in front of the house. I only need you to step outside for a minute. It’s important.”

They go back and forth several times.

“Look, I’m not going to hurt you, and I don’t have time for games. I already told you, I’m a businessman. I want to help you out and hook you up with a part-time job at my store.”

She wonders why he didn’t mention the job from the beginning, loving the idea of working and making her own money. “My sister can bring me up to your store.”

"I'm not going in to work today. I have some running around to do, so just give me the address. I'll swing by, and we'll talk about the job and go from there."

When Kingston arrives, he parks a few houses away, like he said he would. The afternoon is chilly, so Zoe exits the house bundled up in her coat. Stepping out the car, he opens the passenger door for her. The overpowering smell of cologne, mixed with the heater blowing on high, makes it difficult to breathe. He starts the conversation off letting her know his business is very demanding of his time. Then he begins venting about how hard it is to find loyal and committed employees.

By now, Zoe knows Kingston is long-winded and short-tempered, so she sits quietly, listening and waiting for him to talk about her potential position. Twenty minutes pass and he has yet to reach the topic for which this visit was intended.

"You must forgive me. I've got a lot on my mind," he comments.

"That's okay."

This was Zoe's moment to ask what she'd been thinking since getting in his car.

"Can you tell me about the job?"

"I'll probably need a receptionist in a couple weeks. How does that sound?"

With a smile, she says, "That sounds great."

Returning the smile and rotating his body in the driver's seat, he gently places his right hand on the back of her neck and his left hand on the center of her left thigh. She looks at him shocked, not sure what's coming next or what she should do.

Grazing his eyes from her hair, down to her feet, and back up to her face, he says, "I can't get over how beautiful you are. Do you know when you get older, you're going to drive all the men crazy. You could be a supermodel." He continues scanning his beady eyes over her body. "Zoe, I want to help you in every way possible. You don't have to be scared of me. I hope you believe me. I could never hurt you. Something about you is so special. I can see it in your eyes."

He keeps telling her there's some sort of story in her eyes, but all she can see is darkness and emptiness in his. Clearing her throat, she's thinking of something to say to make a quick escape.

"My sister is waiting for me. We have somewhere to go. Um, I'll call you later."

He doesn't respond, just stares at her. Maybe he's biting his tongue to keep from sharing his actual thoughts. Zoe pulls the door handle, it pops open, and slowly, she slides her body from underneath his hands.

"I wish we had more time to talk. I'll be waiting to hear from you," he says.

As she walks back toward the house, she says to herself, "You'll never get a call from me."

☙✹❧

Two weeks go by and Kingston's calls continue. Zoe doesn't accept or return any of them. A few times she sees his car circling the neighborhood. He might know someone who lives in the area, but she assumes he's trying to catch her outside.

~ Twelve ~

Things are going well for Carrie. Her spirits are up, and she has started regularly-dating this really nice guy. Who knows if Charlie has missed Carrie or if he's caught wind of her joy and decided to snatch it away. One night, she needs a babysitter, a friend wants to meet her out, but Maria already has plans.

Zoe volunteers, saying, "You don't have to cancel. I'll keep the kids for you."

Carrie leaves home later that night alone, and Zoe stands in the window, watching her as she walks through the dark to her car, not looking away until Carrie drives off. Zoe decides to tidy up the house a little bit, then feeds and rocks the baby back to sleep. There is a white leather sofa Carrie kept from her old living room set against the wall in the dining room. She hides the cracks in the leather with a thin black blanket thrown over it. Once there's nothing left to do, Zoe lays across that old sofa, talking on the phone with a boy from school for hours until they both pass out.

Most nights, sleeping is difficult, but after so many sleepless nights, her body crashes. The good thing about crashing is her body gets the rest it so badly needs. The scary side to falling in a deep sleep means being trapped in her nightmares, fighting to live, looking at death through a magnifying glass. The torment in her dreams isn't of any specific fashion. She's been chased down, pushed off a steep cliff, stabbed repeatedly, shot, and drowned by waves slapping her from every direction. Sometimes, she's in a dark room with fear and haunting noises closing in on her. They always seem so real in that place between asleep and awake, that place when you know it's more than a dream. A pain remains in her chest from the pounding of her heart. Even after her eyes open, it takes a while to realize she is no longer in danger.

Lying on the old leather sofa, the worst nightmare yet begins to descend upon her, one that causes a gruesome aftermath. The domino effect is one she will not awaken from. Upon the earth is pure blackness, like the moon has refused to shine. Zoe is running as fast as she can through what seems to be a wooded area. Something hard like tree branches hangs over, whipping her in the face and all over her body. The ground departs, releasing her body to a deadly sixty-foot fall. Instead of dying, she finds herself jumping up, running through another wooded scene.

The cycle repeats itself countless times. The last time she falls, a dark shadow jumps down alongside her, shaking the entire foundation. Tidal waves of soil surge like a tsunami. It is just a shadow with no face, reaching down as if it is kindly helping her to stand. The long black arms aim for her shoulders, but don't latch on; then, instead of grabbing her hands, it starts yanking her by the legs. She starts kicking at this thing that is attempting to drag her. Suddenly, it comes smashing down on top of her.

Her eyes close and reopen. She is out of the woods and back on the sofa. Her pants are off and she can't move. Charlie has her right leg trapped under his left leg, binding her left leg and crushing her left knee between their bodies.

Using her hands in the center of his chest, she tries to push him off her, but he wraps his arms around her, pressing down with all his body weight. Clamped in his chosen position, she is mashed deep into the old cushions as he grinds, trying to force himself inside her. She squeezes her eyes shut as tight as she possibly can.

Like magic, in that very second, Charlie jumps off her, like he's just realized what he's done is wrong. He walks toward the kitchen as she snatches the unused part of the blanket down from the back side of the sofa, pulling it over her. She lies there using the blanket as a shield, relieved to have been released but afraid he'll return. Knowing he hasn't successfully entered her, she questions if he'll try to come back to finish the job. Too scared to come from underneath the blanket, which takes away her sense of sight, it leaves her to solely reliant upon sound.

Lying still as a corpse, she scans the house with her ears. Even though he walked into the kitchen, he could be anywhere. There are three ways to exit that kitchen. One way is through the dining room, the second exit is through the back door, and the third leads to the main hallway. In that hallway is the kids' room, the bathroom, and Carrie's room.

She keeps repeating to herself, "This has to be a dream. This has to be a dream!"

The old, rotted-out boards in the floor begin to creak. She squeezes the fabric around the edge of the blanket tightly in her hands, anchoring it to her body. As the footsteps come closer, the anxiety of not knowing what's next to come is worse than the attack itself. When the person she assumes to be Charlie proceeds to walk past, she feels a little more certain this nightmare has come to an end.

Quickly that feeling is stripped from Zoe's heart. The person turns around and now she can feel them standing over her. As if this dream, this night, hasn't had enough hair-raising events, the person takes a seat at the dining room table in the chair right next to her. Silent. Not saying a word. Just breathing in such a way that causes her to be free from doubt that this person's taunting is intentional. Under the blanket, her eyes are wide open in the total blackness. She can't plan; she can't not make a move; there is no imagining.

'This has to be Charlie sitting in this chair. Who else could it be? Carrie can't be home. There's no way he would have done this if she was. But if she isn't here, how did he get in the house? What if they came in together and he's done something to her and now she's somewhere in the house in desperate need of help?'

She feels like a defenseless animal being hunted by a starving beast. Sensing the danger clinging around her, she wonders when and how it is going to strike. This goes on for hours. She can see the room getting lighter through the thin blanket. Her physical position hasn't changed, but mentally, she has surrendered, wanting it to end, no matter what that ending may look like. She needs it to be over.

Finally, the person gets up from the table, slowly walking through the house. She listens until the sound of footsteps fade away. She is almost positive she is in the dining room alone, but still doesn't have the courage to peel the veil off her face, so she continues to hide. The morning grows older. You can hear the neighborhood waking up. Cars are passing by; horns blowing. The voices of people outside their homes. All the noises give her a sense of hope, signifying the beginning of a new day. There's something about the sunlight causing her to feel slightly safer.

Beginning to talk to herself underneath the blanket, she says, "Just jump up and run out the front door."

Not allowing herself to give it any more thought, otherwise she'll come up with another reason to keep lying there, she sits up. No one is in sight. Spotting her jeans thrown over the opposite end of the sofa, she leans forward, grabs her pants, and pulls them up as fast as she could. Her flowery panties remain twisted to the side of her body he'd pinned them to. The cordless phone is resting on the edge of the dining room table. Zoe quickly swipes it, dialing her mother's number in a panic. She wants to go home—not to that place she's grown to hate, but the one she used to feel safe in, the one she still hungers for. She hopes when her mother answers her phone, she'll hear the desperation in Zoe's voice and instantly know something is wrong. In return, Zoe will find comfort in hers, and her mother will say, "Baby, I'm about to come pick you up."

The phone begins ringing, and as it rings, she walks into the living room near the front door. Her mind is so focused on reaching the door, it takes her a second to notice Carrie sitting in the center of the bulky black sectional against the living room wall. She already doesn't know what to say to her mother, and now, shocked and confused, she really is at a loss for words.

Her mom answers. "Hello."

"Momma?" Zoe responds.

"Yes, Zoe."

Her voice turns dry at the sound of Zoe's. By this time, Zoe has become so withdrawn and rebellious in school that her mother now has valid reasons to have a problem with her. She asks her a few questions, none of any importance. Zoe's hoping she'll hear the fear, the pain between the lines, but her unspoken words again aren't loud enough.

When the call ends, she continues to hold the phone to her ear. A second later, a computerized voice says, "If you would like to make a call, please hang up and try again."

Sickness falls upon her, and Zoe's stomach turns weak and queasy. Suddenly, the memory of his horrible smell returns to her, striking like lightning. He reeked of food, alcohol, and smoke, and she just realizes the odor has stuck to her. Vomit starts rising in her throat. Taking a seat at the end of the sectional, she hastily swallows, trying to regain control over her body and at the same time collect her thoughts.

Carrie is turned sideways, staring out the window. Neither of them says a word, but agony covers both their faces. Zoe looks at Carrie, examining her, trying to see if Charlie has hurt her too. Carrie glances up at Zoe, quickly turning away like she is purposely avoiding eye contact. Zoe wants to yell at the top of her lungs, but once again, no sound comes out. Zoe wants so badly to tell Carrie what Charlie did, but with the history of her tolerance for his disgusting behavior, she believes wholeheartedly she will continue dealing with him, which in the end, will make her out to be the problem.

She knows without a doubt most people would believe her, and even though he didn't get in, the doctors probably still could find proof. Although she loves Carrie, she doesn't hold her peace for the sake of her feelings. She is ashamed and feels as though she's already lost just about everyone dear to her. She is afraid the day might come when this jerk's actions could potentially alter her relationship with Maria. There's a strong possibility nothing will change between them, but there's no guarantee and she wants it to be over, so she remains silent.

Still holding the cordless phone in her hand, thinking, *'I have to get out of here,'* she starts flicking through the caller ID, not actually searching for anything, more like fumbling around. She scrolls past Kingston's number several times, then figures maybe he can help. Maybe he'll drop her off at her cousin Savannah's house and she'll have some time to think. The phone rings.

"Hello."

"Hi."

"Hi."

"Ummm . . . this is Zoe."

"I know who this is. What's going on?"

"Nothing."

"Zoe, is something wrong?" He sounds concerned, or maybe she sounds very troubled.

"No . . . umm, I'm fine."

He says, "Oooo-kaay," as if he doesn't believe her. "So, what are you doing?"

"Just sitting on the couch."

"Well, I'm not too far from your sister's house. How about I swing by and you can let me know what's on your mind?"

"All right."

Continuing to stare out the window, Carrie mumbles, "I was wondering why you took off your pants last night."

Zoe turns and looks at her. Carrie refuses to look back, but Zoe knows she can see her staring at her temple.

Then she has a flashback of Carrie's filthy, drunkard man folding her into a knot, smashing all his body weight on top of her. A turbo boost of thoughts followed those images: *'How did you know my pants were off? Did you see what he did to me? Did you have an idea he could have done something to me?'*

The sadness shifts to an anger like she's never known. All the muscles in Zoe's body tighten up. Her heart begins racing, pumping adrenaline through her veins, as she stares at this woman she has loved as a blood sister. There are so many things she admires about her, which made it easy to overlook her flaws. She would have done anything Carrie asked of her. Nobody could have ever made her turn against Carrie, nor had the thought of them having conflict ever crossed her mind. But, in that split second, Zoe's untainted sisterly love swerves to visions of her ramming Carrie's face through the window she pretends to be so fixated upon.

She's forgotten she still holds the phone in her clenched fist until it rings. She looks down and sees it is Kingston.

"Hello."

"Hey, Zoe; I'm outside."

"Okay; here I come."

Before Zoe stands up, she gives one last look at Carrie, who's still curled up in her seat, eyes glued to the window, and replies, "Yeah, I guess it got very hot in here last night."

That probably isn't the response she's expecting; neither is it the response Zoe wanted to give. Waiting for a moment, the anger within hopes Carrie will respond, but she says nothing. She doesn't even blink an eye. Torn between fight-or-flight mode, Carrie's silence makes it easier to choose walking out the door.

Shaking as she tries to hold back the tears, Kingston instantly knows something is definitely wrong. It is evident but he doesn't ask. Turning down the volume, he changes the music from rap to jazz. He slowly reaches across her, sticking his hand between her and the door, pressing the button to recline the seat. As he pulls his hand back, he grabs the seatbelt, fastening it over her.

In a soft comforting voice, he says, "Go ahead and relax. You're good in my hands. I have to make a few stops. When you're ready to talk, I'll be ready to listen."

They ride off in the streaked morning sunlight. The ride is smooth and peaceful, quiet except for the hushed, short phone conversations he holds every so often. Zoe is thankful for the escape from looking at people's faces and hearing the sound of their voices, lost in the world which has formed inside her head. She is trying to find a way through it, or at least get close enough to the front, in hopes of catching a glimpse of this other world—this beautiful world everyone proclaims to see.

Yet, a totally different energy from the universe is being attracted. Her faith is in the world her parents talked of, her teachers taught about—you know, the one described in the children's Christian Bible, with all the pictures bursting with colors and descriptive writing below of how God created this beautiful world for us. And, of all people, she knows she can trust her precious grandmother. She has said it is true, so it can't be a myth. It has to exist, so she prays to God that He will help her find it.

The dream. The nightmare. The hours lying in anticipation. The morning pain, then the rage. Topped with her uncontrollable thoughts, exhaustion falls upon her like a ton of bricks. She collapses. When she awakens, the car is still running, heat blowing, soft tunes playing, but no Kingston. The car is parked in a residential area of well-kept homes. She figures he's run inside one and will be coming out soon. Her body has not rejuvenated and is plastered to the seat as if she is still sleeping.

She imagines the kind of people who live in houses like these: smart, full of happiness, they have to have great relationships with their families and friends. They definitely are wealthy, and more than likely, lucky in every aspect of life. She smiles in her heart at the "proof" that white picket fences really do exist. Zoe hears voices getting closer to the car, which makes her snap out of the daydream. Lifting forward to see, it is Kingston approaching the driver's door, accompanied by a man. They look to be around the same age. A grin comes across Kingston's face when he sees she's awake. He opens the car door, proudly introducing her to his friend.

"Hey; I've got somebody I want you to meet. This is Zoe. She looks like a little doll, doesn't she?"

The man reaches into the car and shakes her hand. "Hey; how you doing? I'm Scotti." He holds on to her hand, staring in her face like she reminds him of someone. "Are you okay?"

She is sure last night's struggle has left her looking a mess, causing him to ask. "Yup; I'm fine."

Scotti is about to say something else, but Kingston cuts him off. "Check this out. I've got some stuff to take care of, so I'll hit you up later."

"Yeah; make sure you do," he responds, keeping his eyes on Zoe.

She isn't sure what it is about Scotti—they've never met before and their greeting is short—but just from the few words they exchanged, she feels he is a genuinely good person.

"Where're you going now?" Zoe asks.

"Well, I'm starving. Let's grab some food quickly to put in our stomachs. I've got like two more stops to make, then I'll drop you off."

~ Thirteen ~

They go to Shoney's. It's lunch time, but they both order from the breakfast menu. He makes a few general comments but nothing really requiring a response. The remainder of the time they sit and eat in silence. She called on him to save her from that awful moment, even though he is a stranger and older, not to mention she previously came to the conclusion he is deceitful and oddly scary. She has no words for him, not because she has every reason not to trust him, but because she is receiving exactly what she feels is needed—placidity—which allows her to do what she does best: go within herself and lick her own wounds until she is strong enough for interactions without signifying any signs of being troubled.

He doesn't pretend nothing is wrong with her by talking nonstop or cracking jokes. It is the opposite of what she's been taught, of what she's become accustomed to, and she appreciates that. For the first time, there is no masquerade, which she finds much more comforting than the clichéd phrases programmed into society and used on everyone in mourning:

"Be strong."

"Cheer up."

"It isn't that bad."

"Let it go and move forward."

"There's no sense crying over spilled milk."

At such a young age, she has already cultivated a heavy irritation for those platituded expressions. Upon leaving the restaurant, Kingston proceeds with running his errands. Each stop he makes is quick, but Zoe quickly grows restless of his many trips, spread out over the city. She readjusts the seat, now sitting straight up. Her mind drifts, seesawing between her own turmoil and the fact that she is riding in the car with this man who no one knows she's with. Becoming agitated, she compulsively bites her nails down to the quick, until they begin to bleed. Not able to rest her back against the seat, she wonders, *'Why would a person have to stop and see so many different people in one day? But, more importantly, how much longer before he drops me off?'*

She doesn't want to say anything to make him feel rushed since he's been kind enough to pick her up, but her body language speaks for itself.

"I've got one more place to swing by and we'll be heading to your destination. Are you going back to your sister's house?"

"Nah; I was going to my cousin's house, but now I might go home."

"I'm sorry for kidnapping you," he apologizes with a giggle. He goes on, explaining, "This is what my days consist of, running around, handling business."

After he makes his last stop, which seems to take forever, he says, "My house is around the corner. I just have to drop something off real fast." Unlike the other times when he parked, he takes the key out the ignition. "Come in. I won't be long."

"Can't I stay in the car and wait for you?"

"I need my keys to get in the house and it's going to take me about ten minutes. And it's too cold to leave you out here."

Zoe hears her inner voice loud and clear telling her not to step out the vehicle. Kingston walks around to the passenger side and opens the door.

"Come on. Get out the car," he insists.

She doesn't want to be rude and he speaks with such command that it doesn't seem like there's much of a choice. She follows him toward a brown building.

"You live here?" she asks.

"Why do you say it like that?"

"Oh, I was just wondering."

She hasn't meant for it to come across offensively, but it's too late because, clearly, he is offended. Zoe assumed all working people lived in houses.

"Everybody ain't born with a silver spoon in their mouth. Furthermore, I'm not into renting other people's houses. I'm stacking my money up so I can build my own crib."

In spite of the fact she didn't mean to insult him, his words are spoken as if it was intentional. The days are still short, and with the darkness comes a cold breeze, slamming into their bodies.

(When Zoe looks back on this moment as an adult, she believes the universe was pushing her, trying to get her attention, speaking to her in one of its many languages. But, at the time, she wasn't in tune yet with the unseen realms of this world. Logically thinking, it was just windy as the weather reporter had predicted.)

Zipping up her coat and putting her hands over her ears, Zoe tucks her chin in to press through the winds. They enter his apartment, which is in stark contrast to the outside. A cozy one-bedroom, designed beautifully, it's obvious he takes care of it with pride. From the front door, you can practically see the entire place. Eyes lit up, he smiles, pleased with himself as he shows her around.

"Right here is Mufasa."

They kneel down looking at a seven-foot snake, housed in a huge glass tank that rims the border of the wall in a narrow hallway.

"Do you like animals?" he asks.

"I love animals, but reptiles are my least favorite," Zoe shares with a facial expression showing she finds the snake kind of scary.

Displaying horror at her reaction, he says, in a macho tone, "Yeah, snakes are pets for real men."

Standing up, he takes a few steps forward, pointing to the right, "This is my bathroom."

Straight ahead is a bedroom, to the left is the living room, and off to the side of the living room sits a small, open kitchen. This place is put together like a model showcase home in a Martha Stewart magazine. It is hard to believe this apartment is being lived in. With no shame, Zoe peeks inside the kitchen cabinets, curious to see if they are decorated as well.

Kingston gets a kick out of this. Jokingly, he says, "I'm glad to see you come alive."

She realizes how ridiculous it may have looked for her to be peeping in on his plates, bowls and cups. Turning around, blushing, she says, "I am so sorry. Everything is so pretty and neat . . . I-I couldn't help myself."

"No, really, it's okay. Believe it or not, almost everybody who comes over, does the exact same thing."

Knowing she isn't the only one silly enough to make scanning his cabinets a part of the tour makes her feel less of a weirdo.

"Come here, let me finish showing you around." Leading her into his room, he flicks on the light so she can see every detail.

"Wow, your room is super cool."

Maybe Kingston wants to show off his possessions, or it could be her nosy episode in the kitchen that's causing him to point everything out as if he is guiding her through an exhibit.

"I have to keep all my belongings in perfect order," he tells her, sliding open the closet door, exposing his wrinkle-free clothing hanging arranged from lights to darks. Baseball caps and his shoe collection are also organized by color.

"Dang, I've never seen a bed like this in someone's house before."

"This is how kings sleep."

She giggles; he doesn't.

The king-size bed sets high off the floor, with eight big, fluffy pillows covered in black silk. The headboard is like a china cabinet, practically hiding the entire wall, stopping only an inch or two from the ceiling. There are glass doors on each side with a mirror the width of the mattress between, trimmed in walnut-colored thick wood. Behind the glass doors are three glass shelves. One side is full of cologne bottles; on the other side lay rolls of jewelry loaded with diamonds.

Mesmerized by the sparkles, she becomes lost in the moment. Gazing upon the jewels as they twinkle back at her, Zoe drifts to a peaceful place inside the crystals. There is no telling how long before her mind would've returned had Kingston not crept up from behind.

"What are you thinking about?"

His lips graze the back of her ear. She almost jumps out her skin, quickly spinning around and facing him. Boxing her in between the bed casing and his body, he stands like a statue looking down at her. Seconds pass, so awkward it feels like forever. Finally, the silence is broken.

"Um, I really have to go home."

"Didn't I tell you I'd drop you off once I finished up here?" Again, he makes a statement sound like a question which calls for no response. "You can go have a seat on the couch." He leans sideways, leaving just enough space for her to slide by.

She goes into the living room and sits down. At first Zoe thinks, *'Something is seriously wrong with this man.'* But thoughts of him instantly fade as thoughts of her returning home come to mind. *'How do I hold all this in and keep acting normal?'*

She goes down the list of people closest to her—the good things, the bad things, contemplating what each of them means to her and how circumstances have changed their relationships. Mostly, how circumstances have changed her.

For the first time since she consciously made the decision to let go of her father, she is being flooded with thoughts of him—memories of them together, standing in the dining room as the record player spins, slow dancing to every song. For the moves she can't do, he stands her on top of his feet, guiding her through them. She begins visualizing what her father is doing at that very moment—

like the way he is living his new life with his new family. She even wonders, if she calls him when she gets home, will he come get her? Will he come take her from this darkness and give her a new life, a life full of light? The light she once had before all this stuff divided them.

It is only wishful thinking, stemming from so many brewed-up emotions. She will find herself in this place many times more—wanting, wishing, dreaming of her strong, fearless father coming to her rescue, saving what no one else can no longer see: the little girl who lives inside her, knowing in her being it is only a fantasy. In reality, she's stopped believing he will ever reappear.

"If I could know where it is you go when you drift away, then I would be able to understand the mystery I see in your face."

She glances up. Kingston stands against the doorway. The beady black eyes seem to have been locked on her for some time, studying, trying to figure out what has yet to be told. He sits down next to her.

"Can I ask you a question and get an honest answer?"

She nods her head yes.

"What made you call me today?"

His inquiry makes her edgy. Struggling to toughen up, she stares sharply back at him to make sure her response is accepted.

"I don't want to talk about it."

Surely he knows how intimidating he is, which makes him that much more stunned by her reaction. Kingston takes a deep breath, then exhales very slowly.

"Well, I want to share with you what my childhood was like."

Looking in the opposite direction, she shows no interest in his going down memory lane. He proceeds anyway with his story.

"I was born in Grand Rapids, Michigan, in living conditions you probably could never imagine. It was me and my two sisters, and my mom really struggled to take care of us. We bounced around a lot. Sometimes, other family members would try to help us, but they weren't that stable themselves, so we all just scraped together and tried to make ends meet. My father decided not to be in my life before I even entered the world." His voice dwindles to a whisper. "I can count on one hand how many times I've seen my father's face."

There is so much pain inside him, his lips are trembling. Fluids rise high on his eyelids. He pauses, taking a moment to regroup before continuing.

"You know, at one point, I thought things were getting better. My mom got married and having an extra income in the house made a big difference. But as soon as we got comfortable, my stepfather died. Shortly after his funeral, we moved to Milwaukee. I was eleven years old at the time. As if life hadn't been hard enough, the transition to a new state brought on more devastation. One of my relatives started touching me. It really bothered me because I thought only girls could be raped or assaulted. I couldn't tell anyone because I didn't want to seem weak or gay."

The wall crumbles and an overwhelming volume of waves of grief submerged the room. Tears pour down the curves of both their faces. Sound is wiped out by the unexpected storm; neither attempts to utter a word. A still moment filled with emotions, he becomes invisible to her and she becomes invisible to him. Their minds and bodies are taken control of by their own individual and most-hidden secrets. Draped on the armrest of his sofa, Zoe sobs until her tears refuse to fall any longer; her face is pressed down into the wet sleeve of her shirt.

He eases closer, gently rubbing her hair back off her face. Although Kingston's story is sad, he knows her cries aren't for him. In his softest and sweetest tone, the same tone as her grandmother's that always melts her heart, he says, "Please, Zoe, let me help you. Tell me what's going on. I promise, you'll feel so much better."

It takes a minute to push the first word out. Slow and cautiously, she begins to share pieces from the most-recent event. She tells him what Charlie did to her the night before. He asks a few questions that lead to her telling him Nicole isn't her biological sister.

"Well, I'm glad you called me, but why didn't you go home?"

Without going into details, she lets him know she has issues at home and needs a little time away from everyone to clear her head. He asks about her living conditions and childhood. She tells him how well her parents have taken care of her and her brother. She talks a little about some of the wonderful memories. Once he realizes she's done revealing her life, he quickly begins pushing for more answers.

"Are your mother and father still married?

When did they get divorced?

Have you tried to contact your father?

Do you blame your mother for your father leaving?

Well, then, what happened between y'all?

What about your brother?"

By the end of the conversation, there's nothing Kingston doesn't know. He wraps his arms around Zoe, she lays her head on his shoulder, and he slowly rocks her back and forth.

Zoe feels like a semi-truck has driven over her chest. Somehow in that painful moment, she finds his words to be true. With every passing second, she feels a tiny bit better just from being able to tell someone. Each time she exhales, she releases steam and the pressure she feels becomes a little lighter.

"Can I use your bathroom?"

"Of course."

Walking back from the restroom, she freezes at the sight of his snake. It has sort of slipped her mind that there is an animal in the apartment. What is equally disturbing is the movement of this reptile. As Zoe steps into the carpeted hallway, Mufasa lifts his head up and appears to be staring her directly in the eyes. The second step she takes, the snake stretches his upper body over to the top corner of the glass tank closest to her and begins picking at the seal. Chillingly, goose bumps spread over her entire body. Quickly, Zoe flies into the living room.

"Kingston, I think your snake is trying to find a way out of that tank."

He laughs. "You look like you just saw a ghost."

"I'm not playing! That snake is going to get out of there one day!"

With much amusement, he responds, "Don't you worry about that. Mufasa follows my orders. He doesn't crush what I don't feed to him."

The voice he chooses in speaking those words and the way his pupils enlarge are all as gravely frightening as the thought of the seven-foot reptile slithering toward her. She feels like she's slapped a brick wall, so she eases into a different gear.

"Um, it's getting late. My mom is probably calling around looking for me. Can you please drop me off now?"

"I have an early day tomorrow. I'll drop you off first thing in the morning."

“I can’t spend the night over here. I have to go home.”

“It’s getting close to my bedtime. I’m in relaxed mood and don’t feel like driving twenty minutes across town, then driving back out here, just to drop you off.”

Moving a few steps forward so she can see the exact time of the microwave, she pleads, “It’s only seven-thirty.”

“You think I don’t know what time it is? I stopped what I was doing to pick you up. Then I rearranged my whole day, catering to you. Now I’m telling you I have to get up for work at the crack of dawn and you’re standing here being inconsiderate.”

Zoe is so confused. She doesn’t know how to respond. The urge to continue pleading with him is brought to a screeching halt. Her blank stare irritates him.

“And you can stop looking at me like you’ve got a problem.”

Looking at the floor until she is ready to try again, she clears her throat and manages to push out a new solution. “Can I use your phone to call somebody to pick me up?”

His face tightens as he stands to his feet. “Your first two rules are: you will never lay a finger on my phone, and you bet’ not ever give anybody this address unless I tell you to.”

His reaction is beyond extreme for what she thought to be a sensible, not to mention common, question.

Kingston steps in front of her, placing the tips of his fingers underneath her chin, tilting her head back.

"Do you hear me?"

"Yes."

"Okay; then have a seat."

Once Zoe sits down, he walks into his bedroom. She doesn't know what or if anything is going to happen, but she does understand he isn't about to let her leave his apartment. She is so angry with herself, and in that minute, there's no room for fear to settle in.

'How could I be so stupid? Why did I call this man? I knew he was insane from the first day I shook his hand. This is all my fault. I'm so stupid! Stupid! Stupid!'

She stabs herself with the sword of her thoughts. Eventually her mind drifts off and she sits in a dark, empty box. This has become a familiar place for her—sometimes landing in a paradise scene, other times finding herself in a blackened, vacant spot, which is just as comforting.

"ZOE! I said, do you want something to eat?"

She looks up. Now he's standing in the kitchen area. She didn't even see him walk past.

"No, I'm not hungry."

"That's crazy how you be daydreaming. Girl, you need to get that checked out."

He semi-lectures her regarding the seriousness of her seeking some mental help as he rambles through the refrigerator. A few minutes go by. Kingston brings a glass of juice and a bowl of popcorn, placing the items on the cocktail table.

"Just in case you change your mind and want a snack before the night is over." He flicks on the television, then lays the remote next to her leg. "You can lie back and make yourself at home," he says, dropping a blanket he's taken out the front closet on her lap.

Maybe the disappointment on her face makes him feel a little guilty. As he returns to his bedroom, after yawning loudly, he says, "Please don't be upset with me. I gotta get a full-night's rest. You don't have to worry, you're safe here, and I promise to get you home first thing in the morning."

~ Fourteen ~

Feeling trapped again as she felt the night before paralyzes her, the thought of running out the front door never crosses her mind. Her head is pounding and her eyes are burning. She leans over, laying the side of her face on the folded blanket like it's a pillow. The only light on is the one shining out the bathroom. She stares at the television, unaware of what's showing, but the people on the screen and the faint sound of their voices keep her mind occupied.

Time goes by, hours perhaps, definitely enough time for Kingston to assume she's sleeping. A shadow materializes inside the yellow box shining from the bathroom's doorway. She quickly closes her eyes.

"Zoe?" he whispers. "Zoe, you sleep?"

She continues faking like she's passed out. He grabs and pulls her hand, demanding for her to get up. Her eyes pop wide open. "What's wrong with you?"

He steadily tugs on her hand. "I said get up!" he barks and Zoe stands to her feet.

She feels fear, not knowing what's happening, pleading to be released. Kingston's response isn't one she would have ever guessed.

"I don't like people sleeping on my couch."

"What?"

"You heard me. I spent a lot of money on this couch and I'm not going to have you wearing down the springs in it."

"Okay . . . so . . . are you about to take me home now?"

"I've already answered that question and now I'm telling you to go get in the bed."

"No; I don't want to sleep in your bed."

Tightening the grip on her hand, he begins leading the way to his bedroom. "I really don't like repeating myself. I'm going to train you how to follow directions and keep your mouth shut."

She's left standing frozen in the middle of the floor as he climbs into his bed. Maybe five or ten minutes go by.

"Why are you still standing there?"

Lost for words, Zoe shrugs her shoulders.

"Lie down so I can get some sleep."

Taking small steps over to the opposite side of the bed, she sits down and curls up on the edge, leaving her feet on the floor. She silently prays he doesn't speak another word to her, prays he'll just fall straight to sleep, prays the night will speed by . . . until her thoughts are interrupted.

"Are you out of your mind? Getting on top of my clean sheets with those dirty clothes on you wore outside! Didn't your mother teach you anything? Take that junk off!"

Startled by the harshness of his voice, she springs up into a sitting position. Hunched and groping forward, she twists the upper part of her body, glimpsing over her shoulder. Hoping he's facing her. Hoping he's found her desperate. Hoping he'll be willing to bargain. But there's no face, only a head of short, spongy black hair. Her throat caves in, her words thicken, and she barely manages to push them out.

"I don't have anything to sleep in."

Taking a moment before responding, never turning toward her, he mutters, "Sleep in your underwear."

Hesitantly, she peels off her clothing, stripping down to her socks, panties, and tank top. Gently, she rolls her pants and shirt into a ball, and lays them on the floor next to her feet. Staying as close as possible to the edge of the mattress, she quickly covers herself with the spread, terrified by the possibilities of all the things he could do to her. Oddly, there's an engulfing amount of shame, just as much shame as fear. Nothing in her imagination of a threatening situation has prepared her for humility.

They lie in a long silence, so long that under normal circumstances, one would be positive they are sleeping. If not for his erratic mood swings, she wouldn't have felt so certain he is also awake. This endless night has become intolerable. Gazing through the opened curtains—the black sky, the moon, the stars, the way they seemed to be looking back at her—something deep inside says, "RUN!" but her legs won't budge. Like a skeleton, she lies staring out into space.

There is movement. *'Did he turn over? Did he sit up? Did he readjust himself?'*

Bones clenched together, she holds her breath, listening for any sound. She feels like the agonizing silence is only a part of his game—that he does something random and shocking, then sits quietly, waiting for it to settle in. This scary thought plants a seed: *'This would be perfect timing for a killing. A perfect set up for a murder. I could vanish with no one having a clue of where to begin the search for my remains.'*

He moves so fast, that by the time the motion registers, he's already slithered across the bed and clamped his large hand on her pelvis. She rolls her body forward, trying to roll off the bed. His grip on her waist tightens, keeping their bodies connected. His heart pounds against her back, beating fast like he too is terrified of something. During these minutes, they are incapable of moving, as if a wizard has hardened them into a solid chunk of ice.

Frozen in this position, she senses Kingston being partially human, battling with the demons that have manifested beneath his external surface. She is rooting for his heart of gold, the heart she envisions to be on the ventral side of human beings. The heart she knows she saw when he shared his painful secrets. Maybe her eyes were deceiving her, or maybe this is exactly how he planned it.

Putting his left leg over her and climbing on top, he pushes her flat onto her back. Humanity lost the battle. The half-smooth, composed character dissipates. Zoe lies still, stiff as a board. He squirms, breathing hard and moaning like she's participating, smashing his mouth into her neck. Licking. Biting. Working his way around to the other areas. He snatches off her panties. His beard is rough like sandpaper, scraping against her skin.

Covered in his saliva, she can feel his teeth rubbing into her meat. She feels like she's being eaten alive by a starving wild animal that has stumbled upon a fresh pile of flesh. She knows this might be the last night of her life, but before killing her, he is definitely going to have his way with her body. She doesn't put up a fight, but she wishes she could be defiant. Instead, she chooses to leave her body. With her absence, there will be less pain.

She wonders if her separation from the act is causing him to be rougher. Or does he become overly excited having control of a spiritless figure? As he rises above her, his eyes are closed tightly; hers are expanded, needing to see what is happening. Knowing the chances are slim, the possibility exists that, if he looks her in the eyes, he'll turn back human.

There is so much pressure from him forcing his way through her tiny frame, her body automatically retrieves its mind, demanding assistance, wanting to be saved. Cautiously, she places both hands between their bodies—one on the lower part of his stomach as a small act of defense, pushing and creating resistance; cuffing and comforting her abdomen with the other hand. Many life chapters will pass and she will continue to hear his sobering words in her nightmares.

"Baby, just try to relax. I need you to be a good girl and relax for me."

In her head, she is screaming, "PLEASE STOP! GET OFF ME." Maybe if she'd yelled those thoughts out loud, he would have respected her wishes.

Sick of her weak struggle, he grabs her wrists, one in each of his hands, pinning them above her head, smashing them into the bed, crushing all his body weight down, smacking against her skin. All her air is stolen. Suddenly, breathing, which has been so natural, becomes a challenge. His torso is much longer than hers, leaving her smothered between his chest and collarbone. At this point her focus is simply on not being suffocated.

She is thinking, *'This is it! This is how I'll die. There's no way I'm going to survive. Either he'll pull out some sort of weapon and finish me off as a part of his grand finale, or he's going to beat me to death by continually ramming his body into mine. If I had a choice, I definitely would have chosen a quick death, but it seems like fate has a different plan for me—something slow, long, and drawn out. I can't take it anymore. He is entirely too big. The pain in my belly is unbearable.'*

❧

"Later, I would learn he wasn't that big at all. I was just that small.

"I found myself staring out the window. The stars sparkled dreamingly, extra bright, pulling my spirit out into the sky. My muscles relaxed, limbs now floating off, captivated, into a beautiful place. It was like the sky took me far away, and I never looked back or rejoined the bodies I'd left lying in that bed.

"I can't remember how long he held himself in that hovering position over me, but I remember him exiting my body in a sad and soundless way. In that moment, I felt like he'd done all he was going to do. The fear of being killed faded away. His energy, his body language was like that of a child who'd made a horrible mistake. For some reason, it now looked like that same fear was enshrouding his face.

"I was even more disgusted because I hated herself for having called him. And I hated him for being a monster. Worst of all, I knew there was a part of me that would forever stay behind. Having any further communication with that man was something I didn't want, so I was angry that somehow we'd shared that brief connection of sadness and great disappointment.

"It wasn't fair. How could he lie by my side in mourning with me?

❧❁❧

Zoe stares up at the ceiling until after the sun begins to rise. He gets up and goes into the bathroom to take a shower. She quickly rolls out his bed, throws her clothes on, then hurries into the living room before he returns. She feels nervous because she's moved without his permission. She is both surprised and relieved when he doesn't say a word. Wrapped in his robe, he walks directly into the bedroom, and a few minutes later, he comes back fully dressed.

Heading toward the front door, in a cheerful voice with a slight grin, he says, "Grab your coat; let's go."

The drive is quiet except for him asking a couple of questions along the way. "Do you want something to eat?"

"No; I'm not hungry."

"What street do you live on?"

"I'm going back to the house you picked me up from."

He glances at her, almost like he's trying to remain free of agitation. Wanting badly to keep from lashing out, through his gritted teeth, he says, "That is not where I'm dropping you off. Now answer the question you were asked."

Of course she didn't really want to go back to Nicole's house. Her plan was to walk home from there so he wouldn't know where she lives. He's probably reading her mind and that's the reason he demanded her address. She doesn't want to upset him. She just wants to get away from him as fast as possible, so she gives him the address without any further hesitation, just relieved he's found it in his heart to let her go. The closer they get to her home, she starts to feel kind of lucky—like being in a plane crash, with the odds against her to survive, but being the one to walk away with her life, without any visible disfigurement.

Before the car comes to a complete stop, she's reaching for the door handle. Latching on to her arm with a firm grip, he pulls her to meet him between the driver and passenger's seats.

"Give me a call within the next couple of hours."

"Okay."

He kissed her on the forehead, then replies with a smirk on his face, "If I don't hear from you, I know where to find you." He stares in her eyes before releasing her arm. She jumps out his car as quickly as she can, thinking, *'You'll never see me again.'*

~ Fifteen ~

No one asks any questions when Zoe walks through the door. She guesses her mother assumed she stayed an extra night at Carrie's house. Going straight into the bathroom, she takes a long, hot bath, trying to process what happened over the last forty-eight hours of her life. She scrubs her body, but with every stroke, she feels dirtier. The only way she could feel clean is if she could scrape off layers of skin, reaching a surface that hasn't been touched. It isn't working. Trapped between aching flesh and grime, she shoves the filthy wash cloth in her mouth, stifling her screams so no one will hear.

When Zoe gets out the tub, she stands in the bathroom for a while, looking from every angle, confronting herself in the three-way mirror mounted above the sink. She pins her hair up in the palm of her hand, pulling it straight to the back, searching for something in her glossy red eyes and her puffy face. Her knees buckle and weaken. It is hard to continue standing, sickened by the throbbing between her legs and the thoughts in her head.

Shutting the room door behind her, she lies across the foot of her bed. The cycle of dozing off and waking up plays repeatedly. She stays in that same spot until her grandmother peeks her head in.

"Are you sick?" she asks.

"My head hurts."

"You probably need to eat. Come on in the kitchen. I'll fix you a plate."

After eating, Zoe closes herself back in her room. The night comes and goes.

☙✹❧

Monday morning arrives, and it's time to get ready for school. Putting one foot in front of the other, Zoe moves like a zombie—dead inside. She takes her normal route to the corner desk in the last row of the classroom; along the way, no one says a word to her.

At the end of the day, she is thankful to have made it through without any teachers calling on her, just leaving her in that invisible place. She wishes the time hadn't passed so fast. Sliding her feet and moving like a snail when the school bell rings, she becomes more depressed the closer she gets to home.

Later that evening, Maria calls, wanting to know where Zoe has been. They're always joined together at the hip, and whenever they're forced to separate, they call each other as soon as one of them gets near a phone. Zoe knows she's been looking for her, wondering what's going on, yet she hasn't given any thought of what to tell her. Stumbling around, trying to shuffle through all that has happened since Friday leading up to this very moment, she isn't strong enough to talk. Looking toward the ceiling, forcing her tears to roll backward, the sound of her god-sister's voice makes her want to pour her heart out.

There's a long pause. Maria becomes even more curious, demanding to be filled in because she's detected secrecy. Zoe can't fix her mouth to tell her about Charlie. Risking damaging one of the few meaningful relationships in her life didn't seem like much of an option. Quite frankly, the event with Kingston overshadowed Charlie's actions, which made it easier to dismiss the experience of what Charlie had attempted to do as minor, transferring it to a totally-different category than the assault that included penetration.

So Zoe begins sharing her most troublesome encounter—the one in which her perpetrator was successful. Only she isn't going to set herself up to be viewed as weak or vulnerable ever again. That's definitely the first lesson taught to her by Kingston, one she will struggle with the remainder of her life. The majority of that unforgettable time she spent with Kingston is told to Maria as it happened, leaving out the details she thinks will make her look like a victim.

By leaving out the description of the manipulation, the pain, and the fear, she's able to transform the memories of that night into a story she can speak. With each word she speaks, she changes those painful images and feelings in her head into a picture that's a little more comfortable to live with. Telling Maria how beautiful his apartment is, how well it's organized, talking about his huge wardrobe and all the jewelry, she only told her of those moments when his touch was gentle.

Being sure to only mention those seconds he seemed human, Zoe leaves Maria speechless; she doesn't know how to respond. She can feel the confusion in Zoe's spirit through the phone. Maria knows Kingston is a grown man and that Zoe has been dodging him for weeks, along with the ill thoughts she's had of him up to this point. Zoe is positive Maria is wondering how she went from one extreme to the next. There's an awkward pause and nervousness begins to break down her phony level of confidence. Truly thankful Maria has held her peace and spared her any further questions, with a sound of reluctance in her voice, she slowly changes the conversation.

☙✹❧

The next couple of day's pass and Zoe feels weird, not actually fearful, but more like, at any given moment, something is going to happen. She leaves home, goes directly to school, and returns home without any detours—hiding in a place she doesn't feel emotionally safe; yet she knows the physical dangers awaiting outside those doors.

By this time in her life, there's been a new belief stitched into Zoe's system. She believes with no doubt there's a monster roaring beneath the skin of every male. In the presence of other people, he's able to disguise himself behind a collective, laid-back, mature attitude. The demon uses his body as a stage puppet, which dances to all the likeable tunes, draped in fancy garments, smiling all the while. Carefully choosing his words, cautious with his body language, it waits for the audience to scatter, for her to be spotted alone, reposed in a tranquil state. It knows the greater the shock it causes, the more time it will take for her to respond.

She can't help wondering, *'How much practice has it taken? How many young girls has it broken to learn that kind of patience?'*

With the exception of her brother, she can see the mark of that beast in the eye of every guy who looks at her. Subconsciously, she's trained herself to see but not look, convinced that eye contact easily arouses the demon living inside men.

Approaching the end of the week, Zoe steps off the city bus, coming from school, headed toward her house. A horn blows. It sounds like it's coming from behind her. She doesn't think much about it until the horn blows again. Now, she realizes a car is slowly rolling beside her. It could be anyone, just trying to say hello. After all, she is walking through her own neighborhood. However, Zoe doesn't want to talk, smile, or wave, so she keeps her head turned sideways, looking at the houses, hoping this person will keep driving. Then the sound of the engine fades. Moments later, a car door slams.

"Zoe! I know you are not about to make me chase you!"

Beyond startled, there's a blood-draining flinch, like a vicious dog jumped out the bushes. Face scrunched up, feet sunk into the cement, she is unable to turn. He grabs her hand, making her spin around, pulling her against his body.

"Why haven't I heard from you?"

Through a whisper, Zoe's voice trembles. "I don't know."

Clutching her body under his armpit, he leads her back to his car. She doesn't understand why she doesn't run when he unleashes her to open the passenger door. He waits for her to sit down, then shuts the door behind her so hard the window rattles. When he enters the car, he is no longer able to withhold the full wrath of his anger. Throwing the gear into drive, he stomps on the gas pedal, causing the car to jerk before he skids off. Speeding and yelling at the top of his lungs, he accuses Zoe of playing with his emotions, repeatedly saying, "You tried to treat me like a one-night stand!"

Kingston merges on to the highway, tailgating and forcing other vehicles to switch lanes, continuing to scream about how ungrateful and disrespectful she is.

Her anxiety goes through the roof. She can't imagine how he's planned on bringing the ride to an end. She starts freaking out, unable to remain silent anymore. Burying her face into her hands, she begins screaming and begging.

"PLEASE STOP! PLEASE LET ME OUT OF THIS CAR!"

Kingston's belligerent actions instantly become physically violent. With her eyes covered, she doesn't see it coming. He rams his closed fist, his knuckles dressed up in diamonds, against her left ear, the bottom of her temple, and the roundness of her cheekbone. The collision knocks the right side of her face into the passenger window. She slides down on the floor, curling into a ball. She can feel the car continuing to move at a fast pace. For a while, she can still hear him yelling, not really comprehending his words. It sounds like a great distance has grown between them. Her ears are ringing, head throbbing, face completely numb. She quivers and tears won't stop running from her eyes. She has no idea how long he drives around or when he transforms back into a mortal. Her eyes popped open the second he lays his hand on her back.

"Come on, baby. Get up. Let's go inside."

She lifts her head as the passenger door opens. Kingston slightly leans in and assists her to her feet. She feels dizzy and extremely confused. She doesn't know if she fell asleep or if she blacked out. As she stands up in the parking lot and notices a large George Webb carry-out bag in his other hand, she knows she's definitely missed a block of time.

They walk into his apartment. He places the foam containers of food on the cocktail table. Zoe's face begins to come back to life. Without looking or touching, she knows there's some damage. As he sits next to her, he digs into his food like they're having a special dinner date. It takes a minute for Zoe to force out her words.

"Can I please use your bathroom?"

Afraid to look directly into the mirror, tears automatically roll down. She can see the left side of her face is swollen and a stream of blood is on the right side of her neck, quickly figuring out the back of her right ear is split open. Taking deep breaths, she guides herself away from any further emotions, remembering Kingston's response the last time she became frantic.

Washing the tears and blood away, she silently rejoins him for dinner. She sits in a long silence while Kingston licks his plate clean. Then he apologies to Zoe for hitting her and promises, "It'll never happen again." He can't look her in the face, so he wraps her in his arms as he proclaims his remorse. "Baby, do you forgive me?"

Shrugging her shoulders, she's too scared to say no, yet there's too much pain to lie and say yes. She can hear the frustration seeping into his voice due to him not knowing her thoughts. Kingston jumps up and Zoe flinches. He starts laughing.

"Girl, ain't nobody finna do anything to you."

Picking up his keys and twirling them around his finger, he suspiciously looks her up and down. Cutting her eyes in the opposite direction, she refuses to give him any further satisfaction.

"Put your coat on. I have to make a run."

The roads are dark. It is a long ride and she has no idea where they're headed, but she finds an ounce of peace in the absence of him speaking. The car comes to a stop in front of a large, old three-story house that sits back on a hill surrounded by tall pine trees and wild bushes. Boards cover the basement windows, and it looks as if the wind has ripped strips of siding from the exterior.

"Come on; you're coming in with me."

Frozen, she gapes at the house like it's from a horror film.

"I said, get out the car!"

Continuously staring, unable to even bat her eyelids, she swallows hard and loud before stepping out the car. An older man, maybe mid-forties, opens the door and welcomes them inside. Kingston introduces the man as his Uncle Tommy. They really resemble each other, except Uncle Tommy is shorter and heavier. Excited to see his nephew, he embraces Kingston with multiple hugs. He offers them a seat at the kitchen table. There's a woman who appears to be his age standing by the sink washing dishes. She's moving very slowly and never lifts her head.

The two men talk and laugh for a while. Then his uncle leaves the room, returning a few minutes later holding a fluffy gold and white cat. He passes the cat to Kingston.

Suddenly a tall, frail, younger woman shows up in the kitchen doorway. Her eyes are red and full of tears. It looks like she's been crying all day, and it seems as if Zoe is the only one who notices her. Just like Zoe's swollen face, the heartbroken lady is ignored.

Tommy walks them out to the car. Before pulling off, Kingston places the cat on Zoe's lap. She strokes her hand back and forth through its fur. By the way it's curled up against her stomach and gently rubbing its cheek on her thigh, she knows the cat is used to receiving love. Later into the ride, it becomes playful and she figures out it's a girl. In her head, she names her Goldie.

Visions of that slender, sobbing woman keep popping into her mind. She wonders if Kingston's uncle is just like him and if he's the cause for her tears. She also wonders if Goldie belonged to her and if she's mourning the loss of her pet. As they sit at a red light, Kingston slants his body toward her, watching her play with Goldie. His eyes light up with a small, proud smile—the same expression her parents had when she opened her gifts on Christmas mornings. Seeing how he's in a better mood, she wants to ask him to take her home, but she fears how he might respond, so she doesn't part her lips.

He doesn't make any more stops, driving straight back to his apartment. Kingston unlocks the front door, walking in first. She follows behind him with Goldie snuggled between her crossed arms and chest like a newborn baby. Once the door latches shut, Kingston doesn't take another step, pausing like he's been frozen over by a freezing breeze. She thinks he's forgotten something in the car.

Abruptly, he turns around, facing her. She instantly moves backward a couple of steps. She can see in his eyes that attack is on his mind. The bolt lock and doorknob press into her back. He reaches out toward her. Spinning herself one hundred eighty degrees, she tucks her face and hides the front of her body inside the corner. He catches the fold of her elbow, instantly ripping Goldie out of her arms and holds her up in the air by the neck.

"You act like somebody said this cat belongs to you," he growls directly in her face.

Goldie is swinging, fighting, trying to break loose.

"I hate cats," he confesses, as if he can't hold his hatred in any longer. He clenches his teeth and blows steam out his nostrils. "I brought this thing home for Mufasa to eat."

All while he is talking, he's opening the lid to the snake's tank. Zoe starts screaming and begging him to stop, trying to grab Goldie. Kingston swings his arm, knocking Zoe into the wall, then droops Goldie on top of his snake and slams the lid shut. He scoops Zoe up, places her in front of him, and holds her in a bear hug with her arms pinned down to her side so she can't cover her face.

Continuing to scream, she asks, "WHY ARE YOU DOING THIS? WHY ARE YOU DOING THIS? PLEASE STOP! SOMEBODY HELP ME!" until he uses his hand as a muzzle over her mouth, smashing her lips in her teeth.

Talking calmly into her ear, he says, "Please don't make me snap your neck."

By now, the snake has wrapped around Goldie's entire body, leaving only the head uncovered. It immediately squeezed the life out of her, thrusting her eyeballs out of their sockets. Blood and meat erupted from her mouth, nose, every orifice. Every muscle in Zoe's face flares; she closes her eyes as tightly as she possibly can. Her knees buckle, her body gives out, her stomach does cartwheels, and everything inside her flies out. The only reason she's still standing is because he's still holding her up. Walking backward, he drags Zoe into his bedroom, releasing her over the center of his bed.

Without looking, she knows he's left her side. Lying on the bed, silently crying, she wonders, *'How and why is this happening to me?'*

It seems like hours pass before he returns to the room. She can feel his presence moving in closer. Zoe's soul fills with hatred, wishing he'd remove her from this misery. But, rather than emancipating her spirit, he chooses to torture her body sexually.

~ Sixteen ~

A week goes by before she's allowed to step foot outside. Her clothing is placed in a plastic bag and taken. Each day she's told when to get in the shower. Afterward, she's given a clean T-shirt to wear, no socks or underwear. During this time, he trans her to be his personal slave. Her voice, her choices, her freedom, her judgment—stripped away by fear. She's taught to clean his apartment exactly the way he wants it. If he feels she's done it too fast or too slow or something isn't done properly, she's punished. The punishment consists of harsh, disparaging words, being choked, slapped, or shoved down to the floor. Sometimes a combination of it all.

Naturally, she wants to please him, hoping to stop the abuse. She figures out ways to reduce the physical contact by quickly adjusting to his routine. Feeling as if there's nothing she can do to stop him entirely, she trains herself to not be surprised by anything he says or does. In some crazy way, the expectation of his attacks makes them less painful. When he strikes her, she grinds her teeth, counteracting the pain by repeating, "This doesn't hurt, this doesn't hurt," over and over again in her head.

This locked-in period isn't only a crash course of Kingston trying to break and mold Zoe to his liking, but he's also waiting for her face to heal. After the first time, he tries avoiding landing the hard blows in visible areas. Even though he wants to hide the bruises for his own reasons, she's still grateful to have her face spared. In between the whippings, the sex, and the chores, she finds a spot near the ceiling, outside the window, or on an object and dwells there, until she's told to go do something different.

There are a few occasions when Kingston leaves her alone in his apartment for maybe an hour or so. She doesn't even entertain the thought of waiting fifteen minutes then running out the door because, in her heart, she feels his leaving is only a test. And the very moment she tries to run, he'll jump out of nowhere and catch her. Even if she did get away, she knows it will only have been a matter of time until she's found. There is no escaping. She can't see a way out. Her world is completely full of thunder and she has no choice but to listen to it and do everything she can to avoid being struck by lightning. Zoe believes his black, cold, beady eyes and every threatening promise he's made:

"'You'll never be able to get away from me."

"I will find you. Your mother won't be able to identify your body."

"Play with me again and I'll kill you."

"You belong to me."

Maybe Kingston's repeated threats are necessary in his corrupt mind. Considering the way he treats Zoe, he has no reason to trust her. The truth is, he's already beaten submission into her body. She wouldn't dare do anything to betray him or go against his orders.

One morning Kingston tells her he'll be right back. Shortly after, he returns with some items from the dry cleaners, handing Zoe two of the hangers. Her clothing has been cleaned and pressed.

"Get dressed," he says.

She quickly puts the clothes on, excited to finally breathe some fresh air. He drives down Brown Deer Road, turning into a Denny's parking lot. Holding her hand, he escorts her into the restaurant. While they eat breakfast, Kingston talks the entire time, which is normal for him. She speaks only when asked a question, which has become normal for her.

Once they're finished, he drives across the street to Northridge Mall. Clutching her close to his side, they walk around the mall from store to store. He almost sounds generous. His voice. His words.

"Baby, you won't ever need anything as long as I'm in the picture. You are so beautiful. I promise to spoil you and keep you looking like a princess."

He buys her several bags of clothing, having her try on each item so he can make sure it fits properly. She is apprehensive about showing emotion other than a random grin because she knows, in the blink of an eye, he could attack her again. Afterward, he takes her to his store, Endless Communications, introduces her to his business partner, and relieves him for a few hours. During that time, Kingston allows Zoe to assist with sales and he begins teaching her how to use the cash register.

Later, stopping by his mother's house for a while, he tells his family Zoe is his friend. His mother shakes Zoe's hand, introducing herself as Billie and his older sister as Jessica. The four of them sit in the living room watching television and making small talk. They stay for maybe an hour or so. Riding back to Kingston's apartment, Zoe wonders when she'll be able to see her own family again.

That night, they lie in the bed side by side. This is the first time he tells Zoe he loves her. She knows he's lying because she has sense enough to know love doesn't feel like this; yet, these three words sound so sweet in her ears. It has been a while since she's heard it from anyone else other than her grandmother, and she hasn't known until that moment just how badly her body was craving to hear someone say, "I love you", even if it is coming from a lying monster. Somehow, it still is slightly satisfying.

He asks her what she wants to be when she grows up. A model, she answers. He tells her he can see her face on the cover of a magazine. He talks about being rich and promises to make all her dreams come true. He discusses his views on family, which is a typical outlook—until he concludes the topic with all the reasons that, in his opinion, prove her family doesn't truly love her. She hears him talking but blocks out the words because she knows he's purposely trying to hurt her. After not receiving any kind of response, he converts back to being a nice guy.

"Look, baby, I'm not going to keep you locked up in the house. I want you to be happy, that's very important to me, and you having an education is also important. Now, if I take you back to school, will I have any problems out of you?"

"No," she quickly replies.

He stares at Zoe for a moment, then slides his arm around her neck, pulling her closer to him. Pressing her cheek on his chest and twirling his fingertips in a circular motion over her back, he says, "Okay; okay." He repeats it several more times. In his voice, there's a strong tone of uncertainty, but a willingness to take the chance.

Kingston wakes up early the next morning and tells Zoe to get ready for school. Dropping her off at the front door, he instructs her to exit through that same door as soon as school lets out. When the bell rings, she hurries outside and Kingston is parked directly across the street with his music turned up so loud the trunk of his car is rattling. They ride around for hours. He makes a hundred stops, parking in alleys, running in and out of houses, meeting people at gas stations. She doesn't ask him any questions because she doesn't care. The more occupied he is, the more at peace she can be. Over the next couple of days, this is their routine. Paranoid an inquiry will cause an explosion, she timorously makes a statement, which she desperately wants him to respond to like a normal person.

"I miss my grandmother. I really wish I could see her."

Silence. She glances over at him. *'Please say something,'* she thinks. Total silence. Either he's thinking or flat-out ignoring her, she assumes. Turning her head, she refuses to let him see her tears. Laying his hand on the middle of her thigh, he finally responds.

"Everything is going to be fine."

By the strong sense of comfort that sweeps over her, by the sudden compassion in his voice and the warmth in his touch when he wipes the tears from beneath the lids of her eyes, at that second, she realizes her guardian angel hasn't left her side. The Spirit touches them both, prostrating Kingston's heart, at the same time reminding her of His presence.

Saturday, after lunch at Red Lobster, Kingston releases her around the corner from her house. He sends her with detailed instructions as she carries a heavy luggage full of terrorizing memories and fears. Now there are new fears.

'What are they going to say?

'NO! What is she going to say?

'How can she act normal?'

These are the thoughts running through her mind as she stands by the back door with her finger on the doorbell. Too weak to add enough pressure to make the bell ring, she decides to walk down the street, giving herself more time to think—imagine, anticipate—what those first few moments will be like, standing face-to-face with her family.

She stops trying to come up with a story because there's no story that will made any sense except for the truth. Lying isn't an option—nor is disclosing all the events which led her to this day. She figures instead of popping up at the door, she'll call first. That way, no one will be caught off-guard. That's the best and only idea she can think of.

There's an older, married couple who own a corner store a block away. They are always very nice to her. She's pretty sure they'll let her use their phone to call her mother, and they do. She feels relieved to hear the calm, sweet sound of her mother's voice. She asks if Zoe is all right and say they've been worried sick about her. She tells her, "Your grandma really misses you," and asks Zoe to come home.

Her welcoming words not only help settle Zoe's nerves, they also put a smile on her face she hasn't seen in a long time. Overwhelmed by the joy of freedom and the feeling of acceptance, she runs all the way home. Being back with her family, even with the existing issues, feels so good. There's a spirit of peace floating through their living space, demanding all thoughts and emotions be directed to an inner happiness for being reunited in a wordless kind of way.

She would have described her own personal feelings as seeing herself lying in a casket, but instead of being buried, she's stepped out of that casket, back into the land of the living. In that moment, nothing else matters. She's happy and grateful to be in the presence of her loved ones and to be standing in the presence of grace.

It grows dark quickly and Zoe's eyes are weighed down. Her tiny body is exhausted. Creeping with the cordless phone into the bathroom, she twists on the faucet, using the water to drown out the sound of her dialing Kingston's number, asking him for permission to stay the night in her own home. With his approval, she goes into her room and collapses on the bed.

Zoe sleeps most of the morning. By the time she gets up, the entire house is awake. As she starts moving around, she can feel the tension in the air. It is thick and undeniable. It would have been foolish of her to not have expected it. She knows eventually the interrogation will eventual begin. She doesn't know how she's going to respond; yet, there's no urge to run. Mentally, she's begun to adjust to one curve ball after the next, feeling her skin becoming tougher. Her wide brown, bright eyes have changed to sharp and narrow, constantly waiting for the next person to aim and fire.

She sits down at the kitchen table, serving as an indication of her readiness for them to unload.

Five . . .

Four . . .

Three . . .

Two . . .

One . . .

The battle begins.

Her grandmother is first to step up to the line. As always, she leads with wisdom, speaking life into the situation. She doesn't focus on where they as a family have been or how they got there, only putting her energy on what they need to do to get where they need to be. Her approach is one that could crack the shell of a terrorist. Zoe's high voltage, electrifying wires are disarmed. Tenseness eases away at the reminder of the power of God. The thought of being able to move forward gives Zoe hope in a way that seemed impossible yesterday. Zoe's heart softens. She thinks, *'Maybe, just maybe . . .'*

The wheels are turning, searching for the right words to get them on to a path—a path that isn't so dark, cold, and lonely. She sorts out the things she can possibly say, keeping in mind the things she can't mention. Understandably, Zoe's eager mother can't hold back her questions.

"Where were you?" she asks, sitting her cup of coffee down and staring into her face, expecting a response.

But Zoe has nothing to give her. In solitude and silence, she keeps her eyes on the floor.

"Girl, don't you hear me talking to you? Who were you with and where have you been? And what about school? What is your problem? Is all you think about is your friends and getting dressed to run out the back door? I bend over backwards trying to take care of y'all and to keep a roof over y'all's heads. You're just like your father—cold, only thinking of yourself. Now you're running away from home. I'm not about to let you push me into an early grave. When I'm dead and gone, you're gonna miss me."

Stuck. Still. Silent. Zoe's tongue hasn't moved but her thoughts have switched gears. Every feeling, except for hope, starts swirling around in her body.

☙❁❧

"Anger. I was angry at everyone who'd caused me pain. Angry because I knew I was losing myself.

"Embarrassment. I was embarrassed about all the things I couldn't speak. Embarrassed because of all the whispering and judgmental looks coming from the very people society had taught me to trust.

"Sadness. I was sad my mother would compare me to my father. I wondered, *'How can you not know the heart of your fifteen-year-old daughter?'*

"Outrage. I was outraged at being labeled a runaway. I thought, *'How can a parent come to this conclusion when you have no idea what your child is going through? Why not think, this is my precious baby and something awful is wrong?'*

"My brokenness didn't fall under the radar of a predator. No, I wasn't simply a runaway. In my mind, those words collaborated with what I already believed, and now, I was totally shutting down. Dejection always immediately followed the mention of my father. I was mostly sickened by all the special and intimate memories because, in my heart, I knew it would've been easier to accept it had he not known me. Puzzled and wanting answers, I needed to know: How could you watch me grow, see my smile, hold me in your arms, fight my battles, dance with me, and watch me sleep—you spent my entire childhood convincing me your love would never waver, then you abandoned me? Yet, I still believed he had the power of a super hero to rescue me, and I had to deal with the fact he'd chosen to not ever reappear.

"When I stood to my feet, I said to myself, 'This is it. I will not wake up tomorrow as I did this morning, allowing my past and my reality to spin me on a merry-go-round. I'm locking this child up. There will be no more weeping. I will accept everyone for the person they've chosen to be. I will treat them as they treat me, and I will not expect anyone to protect or save me.'

"That day, I told myself, 'I have only one thing I will never let go of: the belief that one day I'll be at peace.'"

☙✸❧

She gets in the shower and grief explodes in her chest like a grenade.

Kingston picks Zoe up late that night. He is in a very good mood, bobbing his head and singing all the way back to his apartment.

The next morning, he starts off being extremely nice and gentle toward her. As the day progresses, he thanks Zoe for not making him have to come looking for her, explaining that he loves a woman who knows how to keep her mouth shut because nothing made him angrier than for his woman to put other people in his business.

He goes on to say, "Baby, I'm so happy to know I can trust you. Girl, in a couple more years, you're going to be the perfect wife."

She makes an exit out one door, entering through another. Too young to fully comprehend, yet she can still see the cycle. The cycle of mankind. Wickedness, sadness, and sweetness gleaming through every eyeball she makes contact with. The cycle of secrecy and demons eating away at the soul, altering everyone's thought process. She can see this clearly and strongly feels it in her spirit.

Day in and day out, she wonders, *'How do you find freedom born into a world promising sin?'*

~ Seventeen ~

Zoe's birthday comes and goes. During this time, she's basically going with the flow, trying to dodge the waves as they swoop in, feeling like she doesn't have much control over anything happening in her life. Her only focus is doing just enough not to get scolded or chastised by anyone. She's barely holding on in school.

She starts going back by Nicole's house with Maria since Charlie has taken another break from coming around. Other times, she's with Kingston and his family or friends, and some nights, she stays at home. Her schedule is based on whatever Kingston allows. She follows his instructions without so much as a question. You can't pay her to speak any negative thoughts out loud, even if he's a hundred miles away.

A girl at school approaches Zoe, stating she heard on the radio a scouting crew is looking for models of all ages and they'll be holding auditions next weekend out by the airport. "I thought it might be something you'd be interested in," she says with a friendly smile.

Zoe knows the girl's face in passing, but they've never really talked before. Taking it as a compliment, she's flattered she decided to share the information with her. She's never viewed herself as ugly, and when she sees Tyra Banks and Naomi Campbell—two women who look just like her—it makes her dream to one day walk the runway seem like something she really can achieve. Many things have changed, her inner feelings being one of the main ones. Zoe no longer considers herself to be pretty enough—only seeing the things she thinks is wrong with herself. The girl telling her about that event boosts her confidence.

Easing into the girls' restroom to examine herself, wanting and needing to catch a glimpse of what the girl might've seen, she puts a smirk on her face, then a great big smile, showing all her white teeth. Then she smiles a smaller smile, batting her eyelashes, trying to make herself look sweet. She takes a few steps backward, getting a view from her thighs up, then turns sideways to see the width of her waist.

As the day goes on, she gets more excited. Suddenly, she remembers a recurring dream she use to have of her being a famous super model, dressed in high-fashion clothing surrounded by photographers with blinding lights flashing all around her. The possibility of being chosen by this scouting crew begins to marinate. She thinks, *'This could be my dream actually coming true.'*

She can't explain the joy in her heart at the thought of how her life and circumstances could completely change. When Zoe reaches her mother's house, she calls the radio station to verify what the girl from school told her. The receptionist gives her an eight hundred number to call. There's a recorded message providing detailed information—the address where the auditions will be held, the time, what to expect, and how to appear. She asks her mother to take her and tells Kingston her mother needs her to go somewhere with her, just in case he has any thoughts of locking her in his apartment for the weekend.

Zoe does everything the recording instructs: flat shoes on so they can see her actual height, hair pulled back to give a full view of her face, extra photographs as requested. The ride out to the hotel is nerve-racking, feeling like she has everything to lose and everything to gain. She chews on her nails until most of the discomfort in her chest is transferred to the tips of her fingers. As they walk through the crowd, she tucks her fingers into the palm of her hands so no one will see how badly she's mutilated herself.

As they find their way to the proper area, uncertainty cruises through her body. There's a group of ladies congregating. One of them looks at Zoe and softly tells the others, "She's definitely going to get picked." Although the lady may not have known her kind words were overheard, it is exactly what Zoe needs to hear at that very moment and she really appreciates them. Out of so many people, she is one of the few selected. She and her mother are beyond excited.

For her, it is much more than the dream of being a model coming to life. It also triggers the memory of another dream, one she pushed far away as a little girl, yearning for a deeper connection, subconsciously dumping her entire soul into her father, needing to fill the void. From nowhere, the dream, the desire to have a close relationship with her mother, comes back to my mind. That day becomes more than she ever expected. It is just her and her mother lost in their happy moment, and it all belongs to them. Not only is she her caregiver, but she feels a friendship, a bond forming, and she wants to savor every second of it.

The scouting crew informs them of a second audition which is being held at the Convention Center in downtown Chicago, Illinois. They're told it is a two-day event and different modeling agencies from all over the country will be present. They'll pick the people who fit what their agency is looking for, then interviews will be conducted. About a month or so afterward, there'll be another event in New York for them to attend. Her mother books and pays for their hotel stay.

Leading up to the weekend for them to leave, she starts debating whether to tell Kingston. She wants to share her good news, but a part of her feels there's a possibility he won't be happy. However, she has to tell him because she doesn't want to get in trouble for disappearing. Two days is a long time for her not to check in, and if he starts searching for her and can't find her . . . She knows it will be much worse than the first time.

So she tells him. Initially, he's silent. Then, she's accused of lying and withholding information. The more he continues to talk, the more he convinces himself she's orchestrated some kind of plot, and the only reason she's decided to confess is because she realizes she can't get away with it.

Before Zoe's big day, it warms up to an unusual temperature. She tells herself, "Kingston is jealous, and if he wanna be mad, then that's his problem. Tomorrow, I'll be walking down the runway."

Clouds open wide and the sun fills the sky. Zoe believes it's a signal for no more worries. The day flies by. Zoe is lost in it, with few words, anticipating what every minute will be like when the sun rises again. Strips of shadows begin coasting over the streets, the night turning briskly cooler.

Kingston drives in the opposite direction of her mother's house. Thinking he's making one of his common detours, it isn't until an hour or so into the ride that Zoe begins to wonder where they're going. She sits upright, scanning the foreign scenery. They're somewhere out in the country where there are very few lights. The road shrinks to one lane, with hundreds of tall trees on both sides of them, stretching as far as she can see. Every so often, they come to a stop sign. That's the only traffic control other than the 'Beware of deer signs' which pop up every few miles. There is endless darkness and it seems like they'll never reach his destination.

"Do you know what time we'll get back home?"

"You'll get there when I drop you off."

"I only asked because my mother said we'll be leaving for Chicago early in the morning."

"Did I tell you I was allowing you to go to that crap?"

"Why wouldn't I be able to go? And my mother already paid for our hotel room."

"You follow my orders, and you won't be modeling for anybody but me."

She wants to beg him, "Please don't do this," but she knows it won't do any good.

A knot appears in Zoe's throat, preventing her from swallowing or speaking. Puddles of water reside on her lower lids. Staring upward and out the window, she holds her explosion at bay, watching the tiny stars puncture the dark sky. She repeats in her head, "I just want him to die. Oh, my God, I just want him to die," putting emphasis on it as if she's shooting her wish into the universe, demanding and trusting it to respond.

After hours of driving, even the road grows tired, leaving only dirt and gravel. They ride in silence, except for the crunching beneath the tires, off in the middle of the night, riding through a town so small you probably can't spot it on the map.

Kingston finally pulls into a lot, parking on the side of a cute hotel made of logs. He goes inside for a couple of minutes then returns to the car for Zoe, opening the trunk and grabbing two duffle bags. He never told Zoe they were leaving town, nor did she know he'd prepared items for them to stay the night somewhere.

❧✹☙

When Zoe wakes up, she glances around the room, jumping out of bed and going straight to the window, confirming it isn't a dream. She is nowhere near home, noticing a billboard outside that reads, 'Welcome to the Northern Woods'. The sun isn't shining brightly like yesterday. It's very cloudy and ash gray, threatening the town with a strong storm. Zoe stands at the window, watching as the rain begins to fall, lashing against the street.

Spending all morning and most of the day not speaking except for when he asks her what she wanted to eat, Zoe concludes Kingston has taken her to the middle of the woods for no reason other than being devious. He saw the felicity in her face and detected it in her voice, then he created a plan to destroy her dream. She lies across the bed with a blank stare, looking toward the television, distracting her mind from her heart. She refuses to think about her mother or the audition, and most importantly, she won't give him the satisfaction of seeing any emotion.

The evening begins to settle. In a menacing voice, he says, "Enough with all this laying around; we've got things to handle. Go get in the shower."

Coming out the bathroom wrapped in a towel, she reaches in the duffle bag, taking out the jeans and sweater Kingston packed for her.

"I didn't tell you to get dressed yet," he says, taking the other bag from where he placed it in the closet, setting it on the dresser. "I want to make sure this stuff I bought fits you."

First, he hands Zoe a tiny black-and-gold sparkly dress that is definitely swim wear. She puts it on and it fits perfectly.

"Are we going to a pool party or swimming or something?"

"Nope. I got you a real audition and it ain't no gimmick to take people's money. This is going to put money in our pockets."

Reaching back into the bag, he pulls out a pair of black leather, thigh-high stiletto boots, but not too tall for Zoe's lack of experience with walking in heels. She stands in silence for a moment, holding and looking at the boots that are almost the length of her legs.

"Don't just stand there. Try 'em on."

Plopping down on the edge of the bed, enclosing one leg at a time, she feels awkward, as if her legs are in a cast.

"Let me see if you can walk in 'em."

Zoe stands up and nervously takes a few steps. She knows walking in them won't be a problem. She's worn dress shoes and clucked around the house in her mother's heels as far back as she can remember. Her leeriness is solely about Kingston's secretive plans. He sits in the boxed chair next to the small round table, peering up at her with bloodshot eyes.

"You said you wanna be a model. Well, don't just stand there like you're scared. Start modeling."

Nervously, she takes baby steps. He decides to join in, lifting Zoe's hand and spinning her around as if he's teaching her how to ballroom dance, telling her to be light on her feet, move gracefully, try to be sexy. He trains her off and on for a couple of hours, not allowing her to remove the boots, saying, "You have to break the boots in. That way, they'll be more comfortable."

The rain lulls, a mist remaining in the air. Thick fog laces the woods. Cautiously driving slow as the road twists and swerving around trees where no streetlights exist, Kingston gives Zoe clear directions of the do's and don'ts once they reach their destination.

"My Uncle Tommy turned me on to this place. He says there's plenty money up here and the owner is expecting us. I'll do all the talking and you'd better not let anybody trick you into answering any questions about our personal business. Now, this is supposed to be an all-white club, and if by chance there is a black person in there—female or male—you'd better not say one word to 'em. Your name is Lovely. And, if anyone asks your age, you're eighteen. If they ask who I am, say your big brother. I hear it's small in there and there're only three or four other girls, so it shouldn't be too scary for you."

He reaches under his seat and hands her a pint of Hennessey. "Drink some; it'll help you relax. You have nothing to worry about. I'll be right there the entire time. You are gorgeous and young. I promise they're going to go crazy as soon as they see you."

They stop at a dead end where there are a lot of cars and trucks parked. Off to the side sits what looks like a cabin. There's thumping from the music, but the closed doors strip it of its clarity, reducing the sound to bass and mumbling. Suddenly, she feels herself plunging and she's totally terrified. The air is stuffy and humming of liquor, smoke, and body sprays. Zoe breathes out much more than she takes in, trying not to let too much of it pierce her lungs. Looking less than persuaded when told it isn't as daunting as it appears, the fear rises as Kingston stands talking to the owner. Once he's done, he turns back toward Zoe. Her vision has become obscured as blinding fluid spreads over her eyes.

Tightly squeezing her hand, in a firm voice, he warns her, "You'd better pull yourself together and I mean right now!"

Sheepishly nodding, she knows it is a threat, remembering it is her distinctive aura of despondency that he'd promptly sensed. Hers is so potent, he knew from across the room she'd be his next victim. With that thought, Zoe remembers someone saying, "You can always kill the devil with laughter." Well, she can't burst into a laugh, however, she can kill some of his thrill by rolling with the punches, repeatedly reminding herself of her no-more-tears policy.

A little time goes by before the owner comes from behind the bar to get Zoe and escort her to the dressing room. She observes Zoe hardly moving, so she begins to assist her, taking the duffle bag from Zoe's hand and dropping it on the table.

"Your name is Lovely, right?"

Zoe nods her head yes.

"Okay, we've got to get you ready. What's in the bag?" she asks, unzipping it.

"A dress and some boots."

But to her surprise, Kingston has gone on a small shopping spree. There are several different tiny swimsuits, a jet-black wig with long loose curls, rhinestone custom jewelry, and perfume. In this lady's own unhealthy way, she tries to provide comfort and counseling, helping Zoe into her disguise, using her own bobby pins to tack her new hair down.

"Do you have any makeup?"

"I've got an eyeliner pencil and Carmex."

"Less makeup is better, but I'm going to give you a little lipstick so you don't look like such a baby."

She puts the earrings in Zoe's ears and fastens the necklace around her neck and the bracelet around her wrist. She has Zoe stand up and turn around, staring at her with a faint smile. Then she grabs both of Zoe's hands as they tremble.

She says, "Listen to me, baby. You are indeed a lovely girl. I got in the game when I was young like you. I went to California 'cause I wanted to be famous. A man kidnapped me and chained me to a pole in his basement. It's too long of a story to tell right now, but I want you to know I see me in you. Just like I got thrown into the game, is just as fast as I found a way out. I own this building. I have a huge house built on the lake and a list of other investments. I'm telling you this because if you set goals and always work toward accomplishing them, you will defeat this battle.

"You may need a little liquor, but don't be getting drunk and turn into an alcoholic. And stay away from all drugs; don't dig another ditch for yourself. You have to be alert at all times. Something bad could be going down or something good; whatever the case is, you gotta always be aware of your surroundings. And hear me clearly, you will get a chance to get away from that man out there, and when that time comes, take off running and don't you look back. Do you hear me?"

Zoe nods her head yes. The woman takes a deep breath and pauses for a moment as if she has to force the next couple of sentences out. Suddenly, she's speaking at a much-faster pace and her voice has a tiny shiver in it.

"When you get on the stage, just walk around, then turn your back to all those idiots and look at yourself in the mirror so you won't forget how beautiful you are. And it doesn't matter what happens out there; I'm going to hire you regardless. This will be a safe place for you. You'll never have to do anything here you don't want to."

By the time the woman finishes talking, her eyes are also glossy. They stand hugging one another tightly, then make their exit together. As they walk through the doors, everyone stares. The woman turns, facing Zoe, and whispers in her ear, "Don't go by or even look at that man you came with. Ignore him too. Stay by my side. When it's time, I'll walk you on the stage and introduce you."

Zoe's heart pounds in her chest; her head is spinning with all sorts of loud thoughts swirling around. The lights hanging above are colorful and glow over the smoky, dull room. She slowly walks in a circle, looking at the floor. An additional sadness registers as the thought of her modeling audition flashes before her eyes. Then she looks up and sees droopy, old, squeamish men chasing their youth with fascination and maybe a hint of pity because somewhere inside them is a microscopic conscience.

Although Kingston's excellent disguise for Zoe somehow manages an altering effect, there's still no questioning, with their wives and well-respected lives, that they are aroused by a child. There Kingston stands, directly in the center, right behind the first row of chairs. Balls of perspiration cover his forehead. He, too, looks surprised and fascinated. Suspended in the pool of lights, looking at him begins to make her feel a sense of control. For that moment, she becomes proud, confident, and defiant. His jagged words replay in her mind. *'Yeah, you want to be a model? Well get up and model then.'*

Narrowing her squinted eyes to his skin, her nostrils flare up and she twirls around, flinging the hair. Positioning herself in front of the mirrors, she blocks everyone out and begins auditioning and modeling for herself. Initially, it really bothers her that she can do this, that she can stroll around like a princess, commanding everyone's undivided attention. She enjoys the way the ghostly lights play over her skin, and somehow it feels warm and safe in such a dangerous and degrading atmosphere. Oddly, her reflection somehow reveals to her that she can receive favor in any situation.

~ Eighteen ~

As the months pass, Zoe chooses not to let too much of what she sees get into her head. Still, she feels repugnance and a sense of not belonging. Her spirit is in opposition with her actions and she hopes these feelings will always remain with her. Viewing the principle horrors of this world through an unfiltered lens, she no longer looks at them as a threat, but instead as a circle full of possibilities.

Zoe witnesses an operation, a destructive program, a sickened system acted out by teachers, parents, law enforcers, friends, even religious people: defining human value based on profit or on how nice the gifts are they give. A system that robs children and families of the components they truly need. Everything of significant fulfillment goes ignored.

Zoe has a natural reservation which makes it easy to keep her distance. Overcoming her shyness is never actually accomplished, but it is well-camouflaged because she finds an avenue on this platform for self-expression. Due to people's capacity for such casual atrocity, she feels a tingle of pleasure by returning the disrespect. Her slight cockiness, combined with being wordless, gives an offense that infuriates Kingston. He says nasty things, but he can see they don't faze her. Instead of breaking her, he witnesses Zoe becoming stronger. Deliberately responding to everything he says with, "I'm so sorry, Kingston," she purposely nullifies him.

Despising the fact that the owner of the club is so fond of Zoe, Kingston hates the way they treat her—like she is some kind of royalty. He is outraged knowing he isn't needed, assuming he has unlimited rights to her body. This is the part he loves most—having control, rattling cages, making up his own rules. He finds it to be adventurous, even when there are decisions that don't settle well within him.

When it comes to the south, it is a whole different battlefield. It definitely is for Zoe the uglier side. There are all kinds of people—from the color of their skin, down to feeling free to conduct themselves however they choose. Standing in someone else's shoes, it looks glamorous—live college parties, big-boy statuses, a balling out-of-control lifestyle—that's how a lot of people describe it. It isn't the competitiveness nor the fact that it's a more hostile setting. Standing in Zoe's shoes, it's the part of herself she'll have to totally give up to remain in an environment like that. She can't do it because it is the only part she has left to prove to herself she still has a heart.

She is completely unarmed with the proper weapons and unwilling to be as grimy. Knowing Kingston only wants to break her gives Zoe the determination to fight through the night. The laser red light moves over Zoe's body, injecting her with extra energy. Acknowledging Kingston's black beady eyes on her is acknowledgement that she owns the scene, lingering in every step she makes, as if she's showing him that everything she stands in front of belongs to her.

The longer she pauses, the closer he gets to her, trying to steer her along through the crowd. They keep catching each other's eyes, and in each glimpse, their stares become colder, both allowing a secretive smile to slant across their lips.

☙✹❧

Zoe lunges outside into the night air. It feels so refreshing and pleasantly soothing after being trapped inside that smoky club for hours. Kingston stands at the rear of his car; as Zoe gets near, he pushes the button unlatching the trunk. He reaches for Zoe's bag. She disregards his offer, looking directly at his hand, then walking around him to the other side of the vehicle and throwing her bag in the trunk, thinking, *'I don't need your assistance.'*

By the way Kingston's nose flares, his lips flip razor sharp, and his eyes see right through her, she knows what he's decided, and she knows at that very moment it's about to happen. Leaping forward but not quick enough, he's given her one second and she takes full advantage of it. She jumps out the way, ducking at the same time. By the time he realizes he's grabbed a handful of air, she's already begun fleeing toward the night.

Running like her life depends on it, which in a sense it does, and not knowing what she's running into but with no fear, she runs at top speed, feeling as though she can't run into anything worse than where she's already been. The adrenaline is pumping, and for a split moment, she envisions herself finally getting to compete on a track team. Maybe that thought helps increase her pace, running alongside the cars and watching the taillights flicker goodbye.

After a while, the little red flashing light flicks her mind to a different channel. Now instead of running in a race, she's seeing all she's been running away from: Running from her family. Running from her friends. Running from her dreams. Running from her cousin's wandering hands. Running from the images of what Charlie did and still running from Charlie because he acts obsessed, remaining in pursuit whenever the opportunity presents itself; not sure if he's driven by what he thinks is a challenge or his own cockiness because she's held onto his disgusting secret. Running from Kingston and the world of pain that came along with him. Running from the dream Mufasa keeps appearing in, where he stands straight up, dropping his neck down low with his mouth opening to the size of her head, then jetting toward her face. Running from the belief that she's played some part in all that's happening to her.

Then the panic kicks in, forcing her to tune-in to her body again. Beginning to suffocate by her own weakness, she can't take any more. Her run collapses to a kneel. Hot air encloses her. Coughing and gasping, her body automatically tries to strengthen its lungs. She can feel her clothing pasted against her by the perspiration that has formed beneath them.

It takes some time for Kingston to reach Zoe. As he continues his approach through the darkness, there has to be a voice yelling for him to cease, but he pays it no attention. Zoe surrenders. She waits as he grows closer, then stands to her feet once he reaches her. Implicitly and inexpressively, she lets him snatch her hand, as devastated and drained as her mother had been—and as physically disconnected as her father had been. Wordlessly, she lets him lead her back into that invisible cage he's apparently designed purposely to torture her. His face is glistening like he's been splashed with water; he's broken out into a full-body sweat.

Sitting in the passenger seat hypnotized, watching the cars in front of them, she wonders where they're headed, wishing she was going with them. She can hear the woman's voice from the club hidden in the woods telling her, "The day will come when you'll be able to get away from him." She keeps replaying those words over and over again in her mind, wondering at what point that day will arrive.

When they enter the hotel room, Kingston's eyes are enormously wide and shooting out hell-raging fireballs. Zoe almost folds backward due to the sudden lash struck across her spine. Beseechingly, she spins around with her hands out, protesting the attack. Zoe can't imagine what she's shielding herself from until the buckle collides into her forearm. He swings as fast as a vulture flapping its wings, landing each blow like lightning.

Looping into a knot, trying to protect her face and the front side of her body, slamming the door shut in her mind which enhances sensations, she only focuses on survival, grinding her teeth together, reminding herself of her vow that she will cry no more. Although fluids roll from her sockets, she refuses to join in and withholds all sound. Getting through the first minute is the rough part; after that, Zoe becomes so numb, it's easy to escape the pain.

Leaving him to it, with no resistance, he swings until he gets tired. Once he's done, Zoe rises to stand and stares at Kingston as he walks in front of the dresser, wiping the moisture from his forehead and his neck and the palm of his hands with a towel, looking at himself in the mirror like he's won a battle against Ali.

Zoe picks up her purse and goes into the bathroom. She combs her hair, washes her face, and reapplies her lip gloss. As she walks past the bed, she bends down, grabs the belt off the floor, and nicely lays it over the back of the chair. They look at each other with nothing but hatred, clamping their thoughts between their lips.

Finally, the night comes to an end. Morning comes without a cloud in sight. The sun reverberates off everything it shines on. There's no doubt this is going to be a hot one. Kingston is first out the door. He tells Zoe to finish getting dressed, he's going to turn the keys in at the front desk, and he'll be in the car waiting for her.

Before stepping in the shower, she examines her back. It looks worse than she's assumed. Violent green, blue, and purple bruises. Thick welts, with strips of broken skin dividing them. Arriving at the conclusion that today his artwork will be on total display, she makes up her face and does her hair flawlessly. She loads herself down with jewels and puts on a black dress with a full back exposure.

Bouncing with each step as she walks out the hotel room, her open wounds sizzled as the sun beams directly on them. Kingston stares at Zoe as she spins around like a ballerina, giving him the first glimpse of her show. Then she strolls toward him, modeling exactly the way he's taught her. Face glued to the windshield, his hands grip the steering wheel tighter and tighter as she struts past the front end of his vehicle.

She has been rubbed completely raw, literally inside and out. She wants to share this raw, unmedicated moment with the world. Maybe, just maybe, someone will do something.

❦

One week later, the Milwaukee Police Department knocks the door off the hinges to Kingston's apartment. An army of them, dressed in all-black with shields and heavy artillery trample through his place, ripping it to shreds. She isn't scared; she's happy. This is the moment Zoe has been waiting for—to be rescued—and what better way than by the police force. Kingston has previously coached her through what she's supposed to say in the event they come in contact with the authorities. He's threatened to kill her if she veers from the script and gets him locked up. The plan is for her to give her neighbor's name and birthday if she's ever asked.

Not wanting to alert Kingston, she gives her neighbor's information, but she switches it around, thinking that with the incorrect information, her underage face, and suspicious stare, they'll definitely take her. And she's right. Her plan works.

The officer looks her square in the eyes and says, "Ma'am, we need you to get dressed and come with us downtown."

Being escorted away from Kingston by the police is such a relief. She is taken to the county jail, placed in a conference room, given a can soda, then left alone for a while. When the officers return, she is prepared to tell them everything, but it isn't necessary. They start the conversation by letting her know they know exactly who she is, stating her full name, date of birth, and her mother's address.

Then they begin aggressively asking, "Where is Kingston hiding his guns and drugs?"

She tells them she doesn't know what they're talking about. Unwilling to accept her answer, they start calling her a liar and yelling all sorts of threats. She shuts down; she has nothing else to say. She can't defend herself, confused at what's happening. Turning her ears off, she thinks, *'I'll never be able to escape that man.'*

The detective leans forward with the most-sincere look on his face, and in the most-sensitive voice, says, “Listen, I know this may seem scary, but if you help us, then we’ll be able to help you.”

Tears fall down her face out of pure rage. Staring down at their holsters, she imagines grabbing their pistols and blowing out their brains. But she just sits there in utter silence, feeling the turbulence convulsing through her arteries. They know her age, and when they raided his apartment, she was in a nightgown. Before taking her, she was allowed to go in his bedroom to put some clothes on. They found over a dozen pictures of Zoe and him posing together. Even with the overwhelming evidence of Kingston’s relationship with a child, they choose to ignore it, creating a bigger beast than what he’s already become. By the hands of their injustice and unethical decisions, they too play a huge part in the deaths of the lives of many other young girls.

A few days after being released, she’s back at Kingston’s place. He’s being extra nice, which means nothing because his mood swings are always inconsistent. He tells her not to wait up, he’s going out with Scotti and one of their other friends. She’s standing by the sink when he kisses her goodbye. When the door closes behind him, a heavy weight descends over the room. She feels hopeless and defeated, trapped in a dark, hollow maze without an exit. This life isn’t Life; it’s just something holding her, trying to force her to exist inside it.

Slumping forward, her knees buckle. She drops to the kitchen floor, back pressed against the wooden cabinet door. A broken record of every bad thing that has happened plays over and over, and it won't stop playing. She just wants it to stop. She wants to be set free. Her mind is made up, one hundred percent positive she's ready to create her own exit. She drives a butcher knife into her stomach with all her might, but something hard like a medal armor protects her flesh, preventing the blade from penetrating. She crashes sideways to the ceramic tile. Tears puddle on the floor.

"Not yet. Not yet."

Calmly those words are whispered in her ear. She knows those words don't belong to her because they're the complete opposite of what's in her heart.

☙✹❧

As the season winds down, it seems like Kingston's attitude is winding down as well, almost like something has begun to humble him. Late one evening, in a sad, dreadful way, Kingston sits next to Zoe, choking on his words as he speaks them. Most of it is a smokescreen, but she holds on to the part that makes her spirit rejoice.

"Baby, I'm going to have to go away for a while. I'll help you get things situated and leave you with as much money as I can."

He wraps his arms around her as if she is sad, when really, he's the one who's emotional.

"We're going to get through this. Just do as I tell you and I'll be back home before you know it."

Soon after, Zoe is moved into her own apartment and gets a vehicle as she waits patiently for Kingston to disappear. The last time she sees him, his face is etched with grief, his eyes look weary and swollen, and Zoe still doesn't ask any questions. A couple of days later, he calls from the county jail and says he's been sentenced to two years in prison.

Ten months of his control and not being able to utter a word, Zoe has finally been set free.

~ Nineteen ~

"At the end of my fifteenth year, I was on my own, fending to survive and trying not to lose my soul doing so. I had been introduced to almost every arena inside the plantation I was now wandering solitarily upon. From various sources, people said things like, "The more you see, the more knowledge you'll gain." Or, "As time goes by, the clearer things will become." That couldn't have seemed more untrue for me. With each obstacle overcome and each passing day, things became a lot less clear.

"You can map every detail out. Choose to laugh rather than cry. You can run to the pulpit and let the reverend anoint you with blessing oils. You can sprinkle salt at the entrances of your doors. Burn sage. Soak in the bath with Florida water and rose petals through the most powerful time of the night. But when the sun rises, it is evident something else is also working during that greatest hour for success. Out of thin air, a bodiless shadow swoops inside a random soul for deception, turning your life inside out and upside down for what seems like eternity."

The look in Dr. Brooks eyes show almost every emotion, as if she's just been pushed off the edge of a cliff and snatched back right before crashing. It is obvious the doctor is collecting herself, trying to gather her words. There are a few heavy minutes of silence, then Dr. Brooks wipes her hands over her face like she's wiping the shock away.

“Oh, Zoe, it wasn’t your fault. You did everything you could do. You were only a child. You have to forgive yourself and try to forgive the people who hurt you.”

Zoe continues talking as if Dr. Brooks hasn’t said a word.

“There were no more physical beatings, but it didn’t matter because I’d already been beaten. Injured ego responded by deliberately avoiding anyone or anything that scratched at a layer deeper than my skin. First, I became wrathful, then withdrawn—to the point that people right in my face became invisible.

“The people around me just watched with a smirk on their faces as I descended into a place no child should be. Not speaking so much about the foolish kids and their wicked comments, but the adults who were fully aware, laced with knowledge, yet they played a major part, then they judged me. In my community and in the eyes of my family, I was guilty. I became everything Kingston said I was. His sinister whispers all came true, and I assigned myself to each of those negative thoughts.

“An exile, a stranger, among even those I’d known from birth, at times, I felt the loneliest when surrounded by people. On the outside looking in, it may have looked as if I was withdrawn or secretive. Actually, I was just no longer naïve. It became more and more difficult for me to ignore all I knew and had learned. Out of the need for sheer survival, through the raising of my anxiety and contradictory feelings, I began taking cover in my car. When the air in the room thickened and it became hard to inhale, or out of pure agitation, I would feel the need to confront someone—not with a question, but to yell, 'WOULD YOU SHUT-THE-HELL-UP!'

"Instead of totally losing it in those moments, which were pretty frequent, I began to make up more-pleasant excuses, like, 'I have to run to the gas station', or 'I forgot something in my car; I'll be right back'. Sometimes I said nothing because, if I'd opened my mouth, the truth would have flown out, and I didn't want to hurt anyone's feelings. Although, at times, I had good reasons to be agitated, I understood no one was to be fully-blamed for the battles that raged in my veins. So, quietly, I'd walked out into the fresh air, rush to my car, and lock the doors behind me.

"Soon the discomfort would begin to vaporize. Without truly recognizing or having an educational understanding of the reasoning for my actions, I wouldn't realize until I was older that sitting in my car was a coping mechanism. It became an entrenched pattern used as a tool to stabilize and rebuild myself. Maybe it was the solitude, the locking in and locking everyone out, or the small, cozy, womblike intimacy that caused my car to be the perfect tool to overcome the struggle of difficult moments.

"Then, when I'd return, I'd feel rejuvenated. Usually, the atmosphere would feel different, but if there was some remaining bad energy, I'd feel better prepared to deal with it. So here I was, living as an adult, dealing with real-life issues, knowing I was still a child and thinking I had a lifetime of choices ahead of me. I was disillusioned about my future. At that time in my life, all I wanted was to be comfortable, and I tried a little of everything I knew to get a glimpse of it."

଒✱ଓ

Robbie phones Zoe midway through the week. She is a close associate, and their relationship consists of them coming together for special occasions.

"Hey, Zo, I know it's late notice, but I'm planning a camping trip for this weekend, and I really want you to come."

Zoe tries to think of a quick excuse to wiggle out of the invite, without lying.

"Well . . . I'm not . . . sure if I'll be able to make it. . . but, if something changes, I'll call you by Friday."

"Come on; I'm counting on you being there. It's only be for one night, Saturday to Sunday. You'll enjoy it. Plus, I think a little getaway would be nice right about now."

In Zoe's mind, she said, *'I seriously don't want to be bothered'* However, her mouth said, "Okay; do you need me to bring anything?"

଒✱ଓ

The glow from the skyline peeks through the trees. Her hair is slightly tousled in the mild breeze carried in by the night. Sitting in a fold-out chair, she watches the flames fan out over the logs with great hunger, spitting sparks, giving a miniature Independence Day performance. Engrossed by the rapidly-flapping motions inside the pit, either she wants it to consume her or something supernatural is happening that no one else can see. It's as if there's a voice in the crackling of the burning wood. It speaks a different language, and her spirit is steadied and listens as the smoke tells an animated story as it spirals toward the heavens. It's nothing she can explain other than describing the overpowering energy of serenity. It's beyond magical. She knows she's experienced a symbolic moment, signifying a road is closing and a new one opening.

The next morning, the sun slants across Zoe's face. With a deep breath, she takes in the sweet, baked smell of the earth, and a tinge of joy punctures her heart as she instantly realizes half of what she felt yesterday morning has been chiseled away by grace.

~ Twenty ~

A few years go by. Zoe is still on a bit of a roller coaster; however, she is much stronger. Not knowing the exact target, but feeling in a sense the lane is very narrow, Zoe carries a tactical burden to use everything that has been put inside her because remaining in the ditch where she's been shoved isn't an option. While en route, Zoe pushes back at anything she finds threatening. Hatred flares in their eyes as her determination ripens.

The whispers and the stares add a bounce to her walk. It becomes a satisfying feeling to know they've put so much energy into her, although it is far from positive, and they're hoping she'll fail. She learns how to strut and hold her head up high and smile right through it all. She feels like she's in a barrel surrounded by crabs, fighting to climb out. In the moments of other people's pain, she heard that "light can't take away the darkness", but in her observations, she's catching a glimpse of something which leads her to begin to think that statement is far from true.

It's a warm, crystal-clear-sky summer night; the moon and stars shine brightly, twinkling above their heads. Groups of people, old and young, spread out over the neighborhood. Maria, Savannah, Zoe, and Carrie are standing next to Maria's car. She's let all the windows down so they can listen to some music. A white truck stops in the middle of the street.

"Hey, what's up? It's me, Collin."

Carrie is smiling ear-to-ear. That's the reaction Collin always gets from people. He's a real gentleman with a laid-back personality. She tells him to pull over and park. As Collin walks toward Carrie, he looks back, signaling with his hand, telling the person in the passenger seat to get out the truck. Collin introduces the man as his cousin Jackson. The conversation starts off like there'll only be a couple minutes of chit-chat, then everyone will be on their way. It turns into each of them being comedians and telling stories for hours beneath a beautiful night. All their personal issues are forgotten and they're lost in laughter.

There's an immediate chemistry between Jackson and Zoe. They were raised in unmistakably different worlds, yet gale winds have disembarked them upon common ground. Not necessarily looking, they find a friendship easy to embrace because it comes with no scars. Satisfaction comes from the radiance of their smiles, which they offer to one another around the clock, holding thoughtfulness in their eyes without the urge to prematurely inquire of any painful subjects. Forming a bridge through the sharing of joy lessens their differences and gives an unvoiced understanding to much of their silence.

Their ability to communicate better does not survive the detour which brought them to this place. They tell the funniest stories, smoke marijuana, eat lots of desserts and fried foods, laugh until they cry. That is all they know about each other. Nothing else matters—not where they've been or where they're headed.

In secrecy, Zoe makes time to read and to meditate, and not every night, but many nights, she rests her knees on the carpet as she continues to pray for deliverance and guidance.

ଔ✹ଓ

A week before Zoe's birthday, her health begins to decline. The symptoms start off as a common cold. By the next day, it seems to have turned into the flu. With no weight to spare, it is visibly noticeable that she's getting smaller. Her bones are peeking out through her skin and dark circles have formed around her eyes.

Jackson is planning a gathering for her birthday and Zoe feels horrible at the thought of having to tell him to cancel it. She knows something is seriously wrong. Her immune system is very strong. She rarely gets a stuffy nose, and the few times she does, it never lasts more than a couple of days. With her high tolerance for pain, the fact that she's curled up into a ball, there's no doubt in her mind she needs medical attention. Driving herself to hold off just a little while longer, she's hoping to wake up feeling stronger.

The morning of her birthday, Jackson's uncle stops by. He takes one look at Zoe and says, "Baby, you've got the stomach flu. I've got just the right trick to get rid of it."

He digs inside his royal blue book bag and pulls out an unopened half pint of gin.

"If you want to feel better, guzzle this down. It kills the stomach flu faster than any of those antibiotics the doctor is going to prescribe and it's cheaper too."

Jackson's uncle is an old man who rides his bike around town and gets drunk every day. No one ever listens to a word he says. But on this day, in desperate need for relief, they decide to try his trick. Pouring the gin into a cup, Zoe begins trying to force the harsh fluid down into her weak body. Something at the tip of her core prevents the liquor from traveling through her throat, knocking it along with everything else that isn't belted to her flesh clear across the room, like the little girl in The Exorcist movie.

An hour later, Zoe is at Urgent Care, receiving proper fluids, and after a series of tests, she's asked by the doctor, "What would you prefer, a girl or a boy?"

In disbelief, it takes about ten additional tests before the thought, *'I'm going to have a baby'* actually begins to take root. She is so sick, she can hardly think straight. There are so many emotions. She's afraid of all relationships because of the assumption they always end in disaster. She's afraid of being a mother because, as far back as she can remember, her life has been a roller coaster, and she has no idea when the ride will take a sharp turn, then shoot straight up into the air, then drop back down at a ridiculous speed, only to bend around another curve. All she knows is the ride isn't kid-friendly.

She's afraid she'll end up being one of those women with no identity who lives in the blind spot of their men and children. After stuffing those uncomfortable emotions, as she's learned to do so well, and after the shock begins to ease up, a sense of joy begins to move in. Zoe's emotions no longer allow her to remain sitting in the doctor's chair. She rises to her feet in a lost-in-grief kind of way, holding both hands over her chest, trying to comfort her own heart.

Standing there, slightly tilted forward with tears rolling down, in a very soft tone, she says, "I've been reaching out to grab on to something, but it kept floating away like a feather in the wind. But when I laid my hands over the dome of my tummy, I knew I'd finally latched onto *something that will never fly away from me. In a small space of time, a special love has developed. I hadn't imagined Jackson and I having a baby or being married."*

❧✸☙

Just as they haven't discussed much of their past, they also have shared very little about their dreams for the future. What they offer each other is all they need at the time. Zoe thinks it's mainly because the both know, at some point, they'll be taking different paths, but it brings great comfort knowing their baby wasn't conceived on a foundation of sand because the bond of their friendship is solid. Out of respect for all God has blessed them with, they come together like two mature and thankful adults, and commit to building a life for their unborn child.

For the first five months, Zoe is practically on bed rest. Nothing stays down. If she stands up too long, even her urine falls out. Her body weight drops to one hundred ten pounds. Jackson is so caring and attentive every step of the way, constantly rubbing and kissing her belly, saying, "Please, little angel, be kind to your mommy."

By the sixth month, she is strong enough for them to start looking for a two-bedroom house so everything could be situated before the baby arrives. They find a single-family home. It isn't very spacious, but it is affordable and the plan is to only stay until the one-year lease was up.

A month later, they're moving into the new place, which is perfect timing because they've just learned they're having a girl. Excited to decorate the nursery for their princess, it couldn't have been done more beautifully. Jackson stands behind Zoe with his hands interlocked with hers around the baby bump. They stare at the finished room. It shows so much character; it's dainty, soft, and new. Teddy bears wait to greet her. Ribbons hang, glass angels and glass animals sit on the shelves. Paintings are on the wall. White ruffles around her pillows and blanket.

Standing silently under the glow of her crystal lamp, Jackson whispers with a tremble in his voice, "Can we name her Alysia, in memory of my mother?"

He wants to keep his cry silent, but Zoe can hear it through his sniffles. The baby must like the name because she starts swimming from one side of her momma's belly to the other, making Jackson burst into laughter. He is always so quick to smile.

ॐ✽ॐ

An unexpected storm blows through, which temporarily relocates them to Zoe's grandmother's house. The last day they spend together at her grandmother's starts off being one of the most special days of their lives. Zoe's mother gives them the biggest baby shower, more precious than they've dreamed of. It is decorated like a wedding reception, and it takes hours to open all the gifts.

When night falls and the people have dispersed, they sit around looking and wondering where to begin with the clean-up process. The house is over-flooded with presents and Jackson is insisting on dropping the stuff off at their home. Zoe is telling him it doesn't make sense to take anything else to that place because they've already decided to move before the baby arrives. They go back and forth about it a few times. Truly, she's afraid to go back there, but she can see in his eyes he feels like she isn't allowing him to be a man.

She gives in and says, "You promise we're just gonna drop the gifts off and leave?"

"I promise, baby," he replies, kissing her neck and holding her belly like a beach ball, then he kisses Alysia too. They finish unloading the cars and the people who've been kind enough to help them goes in their own directions.

She tells Jackson, "I wanted us all to leave at the same time."

With a giant smile, showing all his white teeth, he starts laughing at her and says, "Baby girl, you worry too much."

He begins tickling her, forcing her serious face to fade behind the laughter. "Come on; we're just going to move all these gifts out the living room, stack them up in the nursery, then we'll be leaving right out."

"Okay."

Jackson's uncle is the last one to leave. He goes to grab his bicycle out the front hallway and is about to ride home. As they're gathering themselves to head out the door, his uncle turns around and yells, "I'LL SEE Y'ALL LATER. OH, AND JACK, YOUR FRIENDS ARE PARKED OUT FRONT."

Jackson runs out the front door. Two seconds later, she thinks she hears three shots, but it might have been more. POW! POW! POW! is the sound that keeps echoing in her head. Although she doesn't see what's happening, she feels the blows, and so does Alysia, balling up into a knot like she's taking cover underneath her mother's ribcage. Zoe runs out the front door and sees the folding of Jackson's knees as his body crumbles to the ground. She crumbles with him. Her mouth gapes noiselessly, releasing the most somber cry her heart has ever felt.

Zoe slowly sits back down in the chair across from Dr. Brooks. She cries for about five minutes and Dr. Brooks'

face fills with helplessness and sorrow. It is clear Zoe has never spoken of that night as she cries out,

"I've held this minute tightly in my memory. How we held each other's hand as if we were communicating in sign language and as if we knew it would be for the last time. Staring into each other's eyes, I could see him saying goodbye, but I could not say goodbye to him.

"I continued screaming, "JACKSON, PLEASE! PLEASE, WE NEED YOU TO STAY ALIVE!"

"I begged and pleaded with God to keep his heart beating. I even began bargaining, but I guess Jackson got tired of fighting and decided to flee far away from the scene."

❧✹☙

The tightened grip clutched around Zoe's left hand slowly loosens. The wrinkles from the squinting of his face relax. The glint through an unseeing eye records an imprint so deep in her soul, unyielding and taking hostage any witnessing temple. This is the second grenade that explodes in Zoe with a much-greater detonation than the first one. No surgical hospital room, no medication for this amputation. They both just lay stretched out on the hard concrete in a puddle of blood. Her screams turned to a wail.

An officer picks her up and holds her against his chest, waiting as her body convulsively releases a part of its life too. She feels numb, like she's floating on a cloud, just as

Jackson is. She feels totally removed from the scene, then everything turns pitch-black. She doesn't remember anything else about that night.

Life had become so promising. How could the universe commit this ultimate betrayal? What happened is more than a mystery and much more than a tragedy. The nine o'clock news and the rated-R movies inadequately transmit the delicacy of man or of the infection caused by watching a spirit step out its body.

When she comes to, her lenses are blurry. It takes a while to realize she's lying in her mother's bed. Her tears are hot as acid and her cheeks feel like they're burning. Her first thought is she wants to go to the hospital to explain her situation to the doctors. She knows if they hear her out, if they look in her face, if they see her pregnant belly, they'll work harder to save Jackson's life. She wants to stand beneath the fluorescent lights, rooting on the people dressed in all green as they move with desperation on the other side of the glass reviving him.

There is no other option. She can't state her case, or wait impatiently while pacing up and down the cold hallways. There is no doctor who says, "I would strongly urge you both to get your affairs in order. He has six months to a year. Keep him comfortable and enjoy the time you have left together." There is no preparing for his dying.

Zoe lies still, listening for any sound indicating Jackson's return. It is inconceivable, but his disappearance is definitely real. She is reduced to her emptiest point, left with uncut pain, aspiring not to feel. The movement from their once-active baby is also reduced to total stillness. Maybe losing him would be somewhat bearable if it had been an accident.

Some of his family rushes to comfort and grieve with Zoe; others do not. Losing track of time, it seems like several days have passed, possibly a week, then she receives a phone call from Jackson's cousin Lisa. As soon as Zoe says hello, Lisa accuses her of knowing something about his death. She proceeds with calling Zoe out of her name, followed by yelling other heartless comments. Lisa's words are sharp as a dagger. The shock restrains a response, freezing Zoe's arm in an upright position, except the receiver is no longer touching her ear. It takes a minute for Zoe to find the strength to disconnect the call.

She hasn't been eating, and if it wasn't for the distant voices of her family members, she would've forgotten a baby is still inside her, trying to survive. Trapped again in that place between dreaming and awake, something makes her creep toward the kitchen as if she's going to search for food. Instead, she finds herself gazing out the window. She knows it sounds crazy, but Zoe believes he will appear, laughing just before telling her, "This nightmare has come to an end."

After waiting and feeling as though she's been stood up, Zoe lifts her eyes to the clouds and they gather as if they're prepared for revenge. The sky splits open and rain pours down. Continuing to look up without a single blink, she and the heavens cry together silently. Her grandmother appears behind her and leads her back into the bedroom.

When she awakens the next morning, the clouds are circulating, sending patches of sunlight over the gray land. Zoe walks directly into the kitchen and sits frozen in her usual deep-in-thought pose—her left elbow on the kitchen table, forehead resting on her left palm, and her right hand poised on the handle of a coffee cup. It's as if she's looking down a long, black tunnel. Then she feels a gush of heat on the right side of her body.

She looks over and Jackson is sitting in the chair next to her. The warmth beams off the golden light which encircles him like a full-body halo. The size of his smile is larger than she's ever seen it. He gently grabs her hand, leading her fingers to his face. Then he tilts his head, exposing a dark hole where his temple should be. Her mouth trembles and tears begin to roll.

He presses the tip of her fingers inside the hole and says, "My beautiful girl, please don't cry any more. I'm happy. There's no need to be sad because I don't feel any pain." He continues to hold her fingers steady inside the bloodless hollow hole so she can't pull her hand back even if she tries. He whispers, "See? Look, Zoe; it doesn't hurt at all."

With his other hand, he wipes away her tears. His skin is flawless and he feels like silk. She's never seen anything so amazing. It's as if they're both in some Biblical painting. The terror from his murder has almost made her forget the way the corner of his eyes curled up when he smiles.

Without realizing it, she grins back at him. If she knew showing the slightest bit of joy would make him leave her again, she would have kept a stony face.

He begins to fade and she pleads, “Please don’t go,” when she knows he can’t stay. In a sad way, she is thankful. There aren’t any questions about why he came because she knows in her spirit he’s come to bring her some sort of peace. He needs her to be stronger so their seed can ripen. That’s the day Alysia begins to glide again.

~ Twenty-One ~

Where Alysia finds the strength to push herself into this world with hardly any help from her broken mother is nothing short of a miracle. A tiny version of both her parents, she scrapes together the power and slithers through the shadowy passage, a bundle of courage and inspiration not only to exist but glowing while showing her will to survive.

Zoe wraps her in a small, quilted pink blanket covered in little red-and-white hearts. She closes her eyes and squeezes her baby with more emotion than she's ever squeezed into anyone in her life. There's a deep sob. This precious moment brings great sorrow and an immeasurable amount of joy. Nothing has prepared Zoe for the cataclysm of passion she feels when Alysia is born. She opens her eyes and tears begin to roll as she kisses and tastes the sweetness of her baby's jet black silky curls. Scanning her perfectly-formed body and her long eyelashes that cast shadows over the top of her cheek bones, Zoe is amazed by the treasure God has blessed her with. They are one and impossible to divide, feeding off each other and providing the needed energy to remain alive.

When Zoe begins going places, she always receives these apologetic smiles. Other people are full of advice on the proper ways to grieve. She nods her head to be polite, but her facial expression shows she is less than convinced. Then there are those people who want to keep going down memory lane. She views all of it as being disgusting and inconsiderate. Everything they say or do keeps probing the pain. She feels like a militant, completely separated. When she holds Alysia against her chest is the only time things make sense.

As the month pass, the waves don't subside. Not to mention, the aftermath causes a fear she has no idea of until, one day, she's sitting at a red light with Alysia in the back, strapped in her car seat, and a car stops alongside them. Without thinking, Zoe stomps on the accelerator, speeds through a busy intersection, and doesn't stop until she reaches her mother's house. The echo in the silence behind Zoe's reaction expands thunderously.

Sliding out of one groove into another, she never exits as the same person who entered. Putting her right foot in front of the left foot, barely moving, something on the inside insists she go on. Relentlessly going into prayer, she asks God to forgive her and help her. On the way to or from different places, she stops at random churches, usually not even in the appropriate attire—jeans, sweaters, or an outfit that is way too snug. She doesn't care because she's in desperate need of relief. Zoe watches as other Christians walk up, laying their burdens on the altar. At times, she follows, but the ache still resides in the center of her chest. She thinks of asking a minister to allow her to confess her sins. But, then what will she say?

"Pastor, I have sinned, for it is my fault the father of my child isn't here. His death came to me in a dream, but I was powerless and couldn't prevent it from happening. I have no memory of what caused it, however, when I awoke, the need to protect him was urgent. By my own experience and knowledge from my grandmother, I was certain it was premonition, I had an obligation to save him. But I didn't know how to tell him about the dream; I didn't want to scare him. And mostly, I was afraid to speak it into existence. The fitful feeling of an approaching dreadful moment enveloped me.

"That entire day, I could hear a still voice whispering to me, 'Take your dream as a warning.' I knew in my spirit that, indeed, it was a warning. Unable to speak it, I told myself to stay alert and use this vision as the power to untwist the fate which that awful dream had shown me. Later that day, when the sun began to set, two of Jackson's cousins and my brother Jonathan stopped by the house. We had just moved in maybe two weeks earlier, and finally, we were situated enough for a little company.

"We put some meat on the grill and the music was low, leaving an environment for great conversation. There were a few jokes about my roundness, thanks to our expected baby, and with Jackson being such a wonderful entertainer, laughter lived in the air. There was a knock at the front door. Jonathan went to answer it. Before the question, 'Who could this be?' had time to settle, there were two loud booms that shook the house, causing everyone to freeze. Before I knew it, there were two bodies cocooned in all-black with only their eyeballs exposed. Jackson scrambled over to grab me as fast as he could. His arms enclosed around my breasts, wheeling me into our bedroom. Trying to scream for Jonathan, my voice had been taken, or maybe it just hesitated because it was subconsciously aware that too much fuss could cost us our lives.

"By the tightness of the circle Jackson made around me, I assumed he could feel my urge to want to go find my brother. I prayed under my breath that Jonathan had found a haven. At that very second, the power was shut off from the house. We stood in total darkness. Now I could hear people stumbling, and deep, menacing voices demanding money. Soon, there was a set of wild eyes glowing directly in front of me. Right at that moment, a dull light streaked through the curtains, revealing a chrome gun aimed at my head. However, the dull light also revealed a portrait that I saw, instantly softening the wild eyes of this heartless intruder.

"A couple of days prior, I was lying across the sofa, watching a Lifetime movie, and a visibly-pregnant lady's home was burglarized. Once the investigator finished taking the pregnant woman's statement, he explained to her how lucky she was to have survived such an invasion. He also told her the smartest thing she'd done was allowing the intruder to see her baby bump, reminding him there was another life inside her. That investigator said, nine times out of ten, making such information clear to an attacker will deter them from further harming you. The perpetrator realizes they will be charged for harming the unborn child. They can also be sympathetic by being forced to envision their mother or their pregnant spouse or expecting daughter. That Lifetime movie, that specific part, I subconsciously acted out without realizing the duplication until hours later.

"Laying one hand on each side of my stomach, I cuddled my baby through my floor-length, flowy summer dress. As his eyes, not quite as wild, lowered toward my huge midsection, I pleaded. 'Please, I'm seven-and-a-half-months pregnant. It's my first baby; it's a girl. Her name is Alysia. Please don't hurt my innocent child.' Even with his raspy voice, which held a chilling echo, I still could sense this terrorist knew what love was. 'I don't want to hurt nobody. Just give me all your money and hand over that jewelry.' We followed his orders. 'Now wait five minutes before coming out of this room. You and your baby will be safe then.'

"As the thief closed the door behind himself, Jackson once again encircled me in his arms, this time pressing my face into his shoulder, and our hearts beat against each other's. Jackson softly repeated in my ear, 'It's going to be okay, baby. It's going to be okay. Everything is going to be okay.' I felt his words were not only to ensure me but himself as well. A few minutes later, the room door was thrust open. It was one of Jackson's cousins. Relieved to find us unharmed, he let us know it was safe to come out.

"All the light bulbs were shattered. Someone had opened the curtains and blinds, so a little light from the street could give us some sight. We found my brother in the corridor by the front door. He'd been hurt, to what extent we didn't know, until we got him outside and saw a dark stain spread over his entire arm. He lived. The doctors couldn't remove the bullet but they assured him his arm would heal perfectly.

"As if all that wasn't awful enough, the dream continued haunting me. It took a lot of begging and tears and reminding Jackson of all we stood to lose if they returned to that house. That's when he finally agreed to stay with me at my grandmother's, at least for the night. After that night passed, with the help of others, we were able to persuade him to stay while we search for a new place. About ten nights later was the last night Jackson stayed with me. The next day was the baby shower—and that was the night we were robbed of everything: His laugh. His love. His big brown eyes. Even robbed of ourselves, leaving no manual on how to proceed. If I only had insisted we not return to that house, if I had told him about the dream, maybe he would be alive today."

And then, after she shares this horrible confession to the minister, what will he say and how will she feel when he looks down upon her face?

Hiding in the bathroom at her mother's house, she freezes, holding on to the edge of the sink as if the slightest movement might result in her crashing against the floor. Returning to the mirror she once used for so many years to appraise herself, she feels as though her lungs are filling with fluids, setting off a stick of dynamite in her throat. Refusing to let it out, she sends a signal inwardly to bury those sensations. She assesses the pitiful-looking person in the mirror, which quickly becomes a target—forehead too big, lips not big enough, those ugly, faint dark spots left from pimples, the scraggly eyebrows she's sick of arching—so she decides to just cut them all the way off and draw perfect ones on.

She reaches inside the cabinet underneath the sink and grabs the clippers with rage and no hesitation. Not blinking once, she slowly shaves the hair off her head, vigilantly looking as one alien vanishes and another one materializes.

~ Twenty-Two ~

Visiting with her grandmother early one morning, they watch Joyce Meyer over a cup of coffee. Hearing the Word always calms Zoe's heart. Actually, it's the only time her spirit and flesh are in alignment. When the show goes off, Zoe decides to take Alysia out for some fresh air. They go downtown to a mall. It's early afternoon and not many people are there, which is perfect. She pushes her around in the stroller for an hour or so, until Alysia gets fussy. After scooping up the baby, Zoe sits down on a bench. She smiles then giggles when she sees Alysia nibbling on her tiny fist.

"Whoa, look at my greedy little angel."

Swaddling her like a pig in a blanket, pillowing her head on one arm, she uncovers her breast, laying a receiving blanket over her shoulder, giving the baby privacy during her feeding. The natural light beams off the brass-circled railing planted eye level across from them, absorbing Zoe in the elaborate massive glass oval, centered directly above her. No sun in sight, yet somehow, this magnitude of brightness slips out the clouds. A lull intimately glides over them as a shield.

Thinking about the contrast between the heartache of the past and this surreal moment, and the wanting of this kind of moment to happen more often, she makes the choice to let Jackson go. She tries her hardest not to think about him because there is no reminiscing without summoning the horror from that night. A memory, an image, even a thought of him—she pushes it aside, although there's no way to truly forget Jackson because a portrait of his smile and the sketching of his death has engraved a lifelong impression on her mind.

The last time she went to Jackson's resting place, she explained to him her feelings and her struggles, and she prayed always—still to this day—that he'll forgive her and for the strength to one day go back and visit him.

Slowly attempting to put so many things in perspective, she is shrouded by obsession with the battle she feels within herself. The feeling that there are greater depths to man, other than what she's been taught, is coming to her through dreams and visions. The way it pecks at her bones. The way her ancestors were stripped of their daily spiritual lifestyles. The way they were placed in a box by the wage of fear. The way so many religious folks study the Bible inside and out, yet are afraid to teach on certain subjects. Could the brainwashing actually have reduced the mind so deeply that it does not register everything it sees? The fact that she keeps finding herself at this crossroad enhances her curiosity to an entirely different level. She begins to explore astrology, mainly the day, year, and month which she was born, trying to understand her make-up.

In this process of examining the connection between her zodiac sign, her characteristics, and her feelings, she discovers a body of knowledge which unfolds another aspect of who she is. As it turns out, the Pisces symbolism of two fish swimming in opposite directions is as equally-complicated as the planet Chiron. One of the fish has the ability to change its encounters into a continuous supply of compassion. Through helping others, it finds ways to heal and rebuild itself. The other fish lacks inner strength, which allows it to get swallowed up by the trauma it has endured.

Pisces being the last zodiac sign, the end of the cycle, completion of anything, it is always the commencement of something larger than anticipated. At the end of it all, it is great challenges; however, finales are always rewarding, and in this sign, Pisces come to a moment of truth. Pisces are connected to the universal symbol for the divine female as well as the beginning, in which life and light arise. Being in the womb of creation, this sign demands that Pisces bow to a higher power and it will constantly remind them of this need.

Everything Zoe's learned leads to the awakening of something deeper within herself. After being mesmerized for an hour by an infomercial advertising Ms. Cleo's psychic abilities, she goes out on a limb and calls her. There's no way to be sure who she's really talking to, but the woman has a strong Island accent. After a pricey conversation with a wide range of dialogue, she hangs up the phone, convinced the woman on the other end definitely possesses some kind of gift.

Speaking with her at such a weary moment in Zoe's life helps reopen her mind to many other possibilities. But the conviction of crossing a line eats at her spirit and she doesn't quite understand why at that time, considering the

Bible teaches us to listen to men with the gift of prophecy. Out of the fear of God, she never contacts a psychic again. It isn't until years later that she learns the difference between a prophet and a psychic, and she's thankful she listened to her intuition.

~ Twenty-Three ~

One morning, a friend invites Zoe out for a boat ride. There's something enchanting for her about boat rides, and since she rarely gets the chance to go out on a boat, with no hesitation she accepts. The farther out they sail, the sharper the air becomes. She's glad she brought her thick, long scarf as she wraps it and ties it around her head and neck. The waters gently lap beneath them as Zoe stands out on the bow. Looking at the sun's reflection as it hoists itself and sparkles over the indigo water, it's as if the heavens have turned on its sprinkler system and sprinkled down millions of diamonds, creating a sparkly celebration on top of the lake.

Remaining there until the sun begins to fade in the sky, which produces a glow of pink and purple, she only moves when reaching into her coat pocket for coins to throw in as offerings behind her wishes. As Zoe watches the amazing sunset, she stares at a flock of birds flying in a perfect V toward the beautiful coral skyline. A wave rocks the boat, then another; she doesn't choke or flinch at the possibility of being castaway in the ice-cold, deep, wet world below her. She gazes at the undersides of their wings flapping effortlessly as they journey to their desired unknown location. Her last wish is, "If I could fly, I'd want to fly far away from here."

Enveloped in darkness, planting herself in a chair made of cedar wooden strips, pillowed with cushions enfolded by beige nylon, she sways side-to-side from the motion of the waves as it continues to lull the tension in her body. She savors every moment over a glass of wine and cheese before returning to land. Almost everything unsettling now seems to be of the distant past, and some, even of a different lifetime.

On her way home, she notices Jonathan's car parked outside their mother's house. She takes Alysia in to say hi. The house is already sleeping and her brother is about to leave to head home as well. They sit at the kitchen table, and what starts as a short conversation turns into a couple of hours, rambling about work, family, friends, and the future. Before they know it, the second pot of coffee gurgles through the machine. The baby has passed out and the two of them are laughing until tears fall, just like they use to before everything became so complex.

They hear tapping on the window. Zoe gets up and peeps through the blinds. She doesn't see anyone at first, then the motion light flicks on. It's Vinny with a smile from ear-to-ear. She can't believe it, taking a few extra seconds to make sure her eyes aren't deceiving her. She runs to the back door, snatching it open. Both reach out with an eagerness to embrace one another.

"When did you get home?" Zoe asks.

"Today," he responds. "I wanted to surprise you earlier, but I had a few things to handle and it was hard to get away from my family."

Vinny and Zoe have been friends since they were younger, long before complications invaded their lives. One day he just disappeared. Zoe asked around and heard he'd gotten in some kind of trouble and would be gone for a few years. Every now and again, Vinny would call and catch Zoe at her mother's and they'd give each other updates. The last time he phoned was maybe a month or so ago. He'd wanted to know how she and Alysia were holding up.

"I can't believe you're standing here. And it's crazy that you caught me 'cause I was actually on my way home. I only stopped to talk with my brother for a minute, which ended up being the longest minute in history."

"Well, I'd like to think it was fate that held you for me."

They smile and hug again. He walks into the house and sees Alysia sleeping like an angel. In a very soft tone, he asks, "Can I please hold her?"

He holds her the same way her mother has held her the day she was born, then frees one of his arms to lay over Zoe shoulders to pull the three of them together. In a strong, promising voice, he says, "I'm home now and I'll never leave y'all again. I swear to be the best man I know how to be to you both until the day I die," sealing his vow with a kiss on their foreheads.

They are inseparable from that moment forward. He is someone Zoe already cares for and trusts. The certainty, the air of confidence, his no-nonsense tolerance level fits perfectly in their world. He's another survivor of circumstances, searching for solutions and answers for the future. This is a vulnerable period for both of them. Their hearts are softened for different reasons. Sharing a sense of isolation, becoming each other's therapist, they slowly pick over the delicate spots and build on top of each other's strengths. They work overtime putting one another back together; even though all the pieces don't quite fit, they keep trying, finding escapism and maybe a little validation.

Zoe wonders if it's their broken childhoods that draw them to each other. They anticipate each other's moods, never passing judgment, and placing the other one's wants and needs before their own, achieving an emotional closeness more satisfying than they had ever experienced. He holds Zoe and she holds him. They're both speechless. Happiness and thankfulness surround them like air.

Lying on his chest, their legs entwined, their bodies merging, the beat of their hearts is synchronized. At the stroke of his hand through her hair, she opens her eyes and stares up at him—the outline of his nose, the jet-black silky hair that trims his chin, and the plumpness of his lips. He kisses her eyelids softly. She extends her neck, meeting him halfway with a gentle peck. His kisses turn deeper, more passionate, more urgent.

"I love you," he whispers inside her mouth as if he's never used those words before. Although she knows he must have said it many times in the past, it still sounds brand new, like from a place he'd forbidden himself to share. She feels her body has become more fragile than she can ever remember it being. She feels warm, and for *the* first time, she feels safe in the arms of a man. Her eyes close. A tear falls.

"I love you too."

She exhales the words into his lungs. He squeezes her tighter, compressing their bodies, barely brushing his lips over her temple. Neither of them is any longer in danger; they've laid down their guards. They hold on to the silence as if freezing in the silence will allow this moment to last forever, which will not have been long enough. It isn't about sex. They've found the feeling, the meaning of true intimacy, the taste of freedom to completely be themselves. The taste of unity.

The nine o'clock news and the rated-R movies inadequately transmit the delicacy of man or of the infection caused by watching a spirit step out its body.

☙❁❧

Alysia has gotten bigger. She's walking and having full conversations, and everyone treats her like royalty. Zoe always lingers in the doorway of whatever room Alysia is in, watching her playing or reading her picture books or looking at a movie, so happy and secure. Zoe's only goal is to keep a smile on her daughter's face and to do anything possible to prevent her from drowning in tears as she did. By an unspoken agreement, Jackson is rarely talked about, so watching her grow also comes with a sinking heart, knowing a day will come that they'll have to have many detailed discussions regarding her biological father. Tiny. Precious. Angelic. Filled to the brim of joy. There's no way Zoe can tell her a horror story and she knows Alysia will ask endless questions.

Perhaps she also wants to protect herself because she's afraid to go back to that place, to remember that time of her life when she wanted to die and actually attempted to kill herself. It's because of her daughter that she later learns death isn't what she desires. In reality, she's been desiring to have life, and Alysia's strong spiritual intuition never fails to amaze her. Constantly reading her mother's emotions, always taking time out of her busy baby schedule to gently lay her little juicy hands on both Zoe's cheeks and rub the tip of her nose against her mommy's, Alysia empowers Zoe with energy and optimism for their future.

Her smooth, chocolate skin tone definitely comes from Jackson. Her warm, bright smile and dark-brown eyes are just like Zoe's. The sensitive and well-calculated thoughts without a doubt come from Vinny, who she adores. Her makeup is equally derived from the three of them. Her two living parents agree to wait until she's a little older before telling her about her third parent.

By the time Alysia is school age, Zoe and Vinny are expecting another child. From the moment she gives birth to her second baby, she watches Alysia glowing with happiness, proud to be a big girl helping care for her newborn sibling.

'So vividly alive,' she thinks, *'there's no way I'll put her contentment at risk.'*

This is around the time she realizes it will be much longer before she can begin to attempt to talk about Jackson. She fears at some point the devil will swoop in and use their painful past to attack their angel, like a Chihuahua snapping and latching its sharp teeth into your skin every chance it gets. Zoe hopes she can just get Alysia through her childhood and through school without causing her to have to deal with something so devastating. Because if anything happens to Alysia, like what had happened to Zoe, helping her will be much more challenging if she's already in a state of withdrawal or isolation or shutting down.

Zoe knows her decision is a double-edged sword because she knows, one day in the future, her beautiful daughter will look her square in her face with great disappointment and say, "But, Mommy, you deprived me of something I had the right to know." And there is always the thought, *'What if she never forgives me?'* that hovers in the corner of her mind. She won't allow these negative thoughts to take her captive because she believes, wholeheartedly, that if she does her part, God will bring them even closer.

Even with Zoe's faith, this is no easy thing to live with. It mixes in the pot of her gut with all the other toxins stirring around, slowly eating her alive. This isn't one of those situations you can train yourself to handle by denial, and it isn't a black-or-white issue with a right-or-wrong solution. There aren't any correct answers, just taking steps one day at a time, weighing out the pros and cons, following the guide designed by the world which is placed in her hands. So she prays for her babies and she prays with them. She begins giving them spiritual baths and preparing them to have intellectual conversations, training them to be compassionate, understanding, sympathetic, and to think with wisdom. Together, she and Vinny put the best of themselves into their children, shielding while equipping them to be successful as well as at peace with themselves.

~ Twenty-Four ~

Overall, things are operating well. Zoe believes she now has most of her inner issues somewhat under control. She's bought a newly-remodeled home, then decided she's done working for other people. With her mother's help, she's able to get her first business started. Zoe and Vinny are put under scrutiny. Zoe is sure a couple of people are genuinely supportive and rooting for them. Then there's the group that's bitterly unhappy with their own lives, so negativity naturally consumes them. Some grow profoundly silent. Others pick at them—poking, pulling, stretching—fully aware they are already broken. Deceitful plots and lies, and when one thing doesn't work, they try another, causing it to be almost impossible for them to make it out together.

Thinking she has to fight for herself, because she was taught to fight, and accustomed to being abandoned and fending for herself, she begins thinking he isn't being a good protector. Every other day, it's something else unwarranted. She's been defending herself for so long, she isn't healthy enough to maturely respond to the strikes. Unfortunately, they also reinforce her sense of inadequacy and the entrapment of her own personal battles. Her attitude says, "You don't have to like me, but I've been through too much to accept you attacking me."

She fires back every chance she gets. Things get so bad Vinny's uncle gets involved. He's a reasonable man, kind of like the family mediator. She explains to him what's happening, completing the parts of the stories that have been left untold. His uncle pauses for a second, taking it all in. Finally, he responds.

"Look, the real problem is Vinny was gone for five years. They had an extremely close bond with him. They missed him and they want him back. It's as simple as that."

Realistically, Zoe knows that's where the problem originally stemmed from. She's known these guys for years and has never had an issue with any of them. It doesn't matter who's right or wrong because, in the end, she turns out to be one of them. Only they are successful and confrontations crack their foundation. Now, everybody is being driven by anger or some sort of evil source. Nobody has been trained to properly articulate their voice.

They throw every trick they have at them—playing games, lying, and disrespecting her and Vinny. She is so tired of being crushed from every direction of life, she can't control her alter ego. She has to keep fighting back, feeling as though she has to prove her humanity. They all have been raised in broken homes, and it has nearly destroyed each of them. She can't understand how they find pleasure in tearing down her kids' family.

Things rapidly begin to change. One minute, Zoe and Vinny are all over each other, laughing and planning their futures with so much to gain. Holding one another in the bathtub with body oils and overflowing with bubbles, surrounded by scented candles. The next minute, they're both protesting.

Vinny and Zoe have both suffered from many traumatic events, but, of course, they are all dismissed or considered minor. Or the famous line will be quoted, "That ain't got nothing to do with you," which is crazy since any interruption causes such an eruption in the lives they've fought for daily to be triumphant. The extrasensory, funded by the personal history carved into their hearts, effectuates the mood swings.

"I love you."

"I can't live without you."

"I know I've said sorry before, but this time it's true."

Then they discuss marriage over steak, potatoes, eggs, and juice.

A week or so goes by.

"Is there another woman? Because I refuse to share you."

"I saw the name Brian in your contact list. Let's talk about him too."

"I'm going out with the guys; don't wait up."

"Cool."

Then she jumps on the phone, calling Savannah as she does her hair and makeup.

Three o'clock in the morning. Now they're making love; no recollection that they were just on the verge of breaking up.

ঔ✹ঌ

A Month Later . . .

"You don't love me. You love being in the streets."

"Stay in a woman's place and quit trying to change me."

"If there is no equality, there's no us."

"Take these few dollars; go have some fun."

"I hate you."

"Yeah, sweets; I love you too."

This becomes the lyrics to their tune.

Maybe he is a man, but she's a woman. Every cruel word, every thoughtless action further opens the wounds to their old coping habits. At times, they love each other obsessively, which makes them fight to prove neither of them is weak. The perimeters for the things they'll say or not say spreads as wide as a football field. They become more committed to being right than being in harmony, both transcending into professionals at pushing the other's buttons, then acting like the other one is the psycho.

One day they are arguing. She knows how he feels about being challenged, especially by his woman, but she's been quiet enough and she isn't going to shut up. Vinny's face screams danger. She thinks of Kingston and of how defenseless she used to be. A wave of electricity shoots through her body and she says to herself, "Never again will a man control me."

They act out the only way they know how. Unlike her mother, Zoe doesn't have the guts to start over. Just like her father, it's evident the intent isn't to cause physical damage but to conquer psychological submission.

"Sweets, I'm sorry. Sweets, I'm so sorry."

It is too late; the switch has been flipped. How much miscommunication it must have taken for them to shift from there to here. This level of disrespect. This level of distrust. How did this happen between two people whose love could never be reciprocated?

Sometimes she thinks they might have made it, if they'd been wise enough, strong enough to take a time out and deal with their individual hang-ups. Instead, they stayed in this unhealthy rotation, with family members wickedly intervening, as if they can't find enough satisfaction in all the other issues they'd already caused. Staying together, they separately battled their own repressions, being overly-demanding of each other, not allowing divine order to take its course.

Then one day, it is the stunning blow of her realizing she is no longer a priority. It's as if the wounds are taking shape in her eyes. It is the fact of her being without a voice that knocks her down for the count.

Zoe yells, “Get out! Just stay away from me!”

He yells, “Baby, I love you. Why can’t you trust me and see things my way?”

“No, you love money and the excitement of the street, and I can’t be the kind of woman you want me to be.”

“Everything I do is for us. Why can’t you just be happy and support me?”

“I can’t take it any more. I want you to go.”

Zoe drops to her knees as if begging to be freed.

He collapses in front of her and says, “Fine; I’ll leave.”

Just like the first night when they said they loved each other, he holds her, she holds him. They both are speechless. Bodies entwine and the beat of their hearts is still synchronized, but this time they’re mourning, faces covered in tears. They unlock and leave the door open, welcoming other people to enter their web. Now they are quick to find a double meaning in everything they say to one another. Frowning becomes automatic. Each is aware of the heart resting deeply in the other one’s eyes. They try hard not to display a demeanor of them still being in love. Neither wants to give up their pridefulness.

Hearing the sound of air being sucked through people’s teeth, they begin to embrace in secrecy, hiding from their opponents’ disapproval, lost in mayhem, tangled in all sorts of feelings. Somewhere between the tits-for-tats, something similar to hatred slides in. They no longer make love; it's more like a quest for affirmation. Both possessing deadly seeds, they water them and the people around them watch them grow, and by solemn command of their flesh, they can't resist the cravings.

Because Zoe is a little girl, a daughter who longs for and desperately needs her father, she feels like she has to open the door every time Vinny comes knocking. Only a small percentage is for affection; the rest is her giving herself up to give her children back their daddy. Her best friend, her lover has suddenly become a stranger. It is a major hurdle. The trouble is she genuinely has good reasons for her emotions, as he does as well. Zoe believes they both know they've done some things they can't come back from, but having a piece of each other is better than losing each other all together, so he keeps one foot in the door and she never pushes it completely out.

Years of trying to separate brings about a sorrow more protracted than she's suffered in the past because, every time she starts to heal, the stitches are abruptly ripped out, leaving a deeper gash than before.

There's an older woman who lives directly across the street from Zoe. By the ages of her children and her appearance, Zoe guesses she's somewhere in her early sixties. From the very first day she moves in the house, this woman begins boldly trying to push her way into Zoe's space. The movers haven't finished unloading the U-Haul and Zoe runs outside to get something from the back seat of her car. As she pulls the top of her body from the vehicle, rising to a stand with a box of flowers enclosed in her arms, she has no idea someone is standing behind her.

"I saw you looking around the outside of this house the day it went on the market."

Startled by the closeness of this faceless voice, Zoe almost jumps out her skin as she quickly spins around.

"Oh, I'm sorry. I didn't mean to sneak up on you. Just thought I'd catch you and welcome you into the neighborhood."

The woman has a smile on her face but her eyes say something else. Zoe clamps her lips together for a second, stopping her thoughts from exiting her mouth. She closes the car door, and with a confused look on her face, she finally responds. "Thank you," and not a word more as she instantly turns and walks away.

She isn't sure if it's the woman's words, the feeling she intentionally crept up on her, or the fact that her face and her words tell two different stories, but whatever the case, she can't shake the eerie chill crawling through her body. She tries to eject the uneasiness by telling herself, "It is dark in a new environment. She just caught me off guard."

It becomes harder not to be bothered once it's evident the woman is watching her every chance she gets, sitting in the corner on her porch, surrounded by tall plants and hanging flowers with long vines and wild untrimmed brushes, staying hidden from the naked eye. Spending her days living as a spy, she spends years of purposely dodging this woman.

One day, Zoe is unloading groceries from the trunk, and the woman pulls up and parks in front of Zoe's car. *'Ugh, man! All that space across the street in front of her own house, but she's got to park right here,'* Zoe thinks. "Please don't say anything to me," she keeps repeating to herself, probably because, in her gut, she knows this woman has been waiting on an opportunity to get in her face. As soon as Zoe shuts the trunk, there the woman is, with a smile on her lips and eyes squinted, shooting sharp arrows like a murderer on the hunt.

"You're always on the run. Business must be doing well."

"I can't complain."

"Oh well, that's good to hear because I've had you in my thoughts for a few days now, ever since I saw that man of yours moving out. You know, it's a real shame families can't learn to stay together."

Zoe takes a deep breath. "Yes, you're right about that."

"I've been noticing you and your family doing some work on that restaurant around the corner. Ummm, I hear you're getting ready for a grand opening. So, what kind of food you plan on serving?"

Trying to keep a pleasant expression, Zoe replies, "The menu isn't completed." Zoe steps to the right as if she's going to walk around the woman. “I’m sorry, I have to get these bags in the house and go pick up my kids.”

“Yeah, I’m sure you do, but before you go, I wanted to let you know I’ve had cameras installed all around the exterior of my home and they’re pointing in every direction. Don’t nothing get past me. I see everything. I know what time people come and go. I even see what’s going on during the hours folks should be sleep.”

As if the woman’s smile can’t be more haunting, she pokes her lips out and the edges of her mouth curl up like the Joker’s. Zoe proceeds to ease away like the woman has a contagious disease.

One afternoon, Zoe returns home with her friend Chloe. (They’d met some years back in their early twenties, working in the same department of a retail corporate office.) As they walk up the concrete stairs approaching the front door, they are shocked to see raw eggs splattered against Zoe’s bedroom window. Chloe immediately becomes furious.

“These kids nowadays need their butts whupped, running around vandalizing people’s property.”

Zoe stares up at the dripping yokes, looking less than convinced. “But why would some kids do this?”

“Girl, because they don’t have any home training, that’s why.”

She glances over her yard, clearly unsettled with her friend’s assumption.

"Chloe, look at how big this tree is. There's no way those eggs were thrown from the sidewalk." Then she peeks around the side of her house. "And the security fence is locked. That means, some kids walked straight up in the front of my yard in broad daylight, and from a close range, threw the eggs high enough to hit the window on the second floor. And why did all the eggs only land on the window to my bedroom?"

"I guess since you put it like that, it does seem kind of weird, but who other than kids would be throwing eggs?"

"Yeah, maybe you're right," Zoe mumbles as she enters her home, less bothered by the vandalism and more bothered by the unexplainable hunch that she was targeted for an unknown reason.

~ Twenty-Five ~

Zoe fights to rise above the statistics, while trying to assert liveliness into her children. Working nonstop, adjusting to only a few hours of rest, she is sure to set aside a block of time for primping so she can fiercely share a wink with society. She crosses out any reason to grieve simply because she's grieved enough, which results in lowering her expectations and expecting a less-than-part-time relationship from Vinny.

She justified it to herself by saying, "I'll give him what he wants as long as he gives me what I want, and together, we'll give the kids what they want. Then everybody should be happy."

She's striving to be better, while holding on to a slave's mentality. When many of our ancestors were set free after being oppressed for so long, they chose to remain servants, due to their lack of self-worth and the forceful indoctrination that had caused them to willingly accept being subjected to major discomfort. They were rewarded with shelter and extremely small tokens, depending on the day of the week, to go along with their master's operation. Somehow that becomes Zoe.

Zoe starts to have recurring dreams of faceless people dressed in black leotards crawling through the picture-sized windows of her living room and dining room. The dreams are so real they shock her all the way out of her sleep. She carries the fear from those dreams through the entire day—maybe because the windows rest only a couple of feet above the flower beds and someone could actually crawl in. She convinces herself that subconsciously she's causing the dreams now that Vinny isn't staying there every night, and from the outside looking in, it might appear she has valuables in her possession. She concludes the dreams are in connection to her paranoia.

She recalls the day she signed the closing papers and received the keys. She was dolled up in a black-and-white pants suit and Maria met her at the house. She loved it just as much as Zoe. She took pictures of Zoe pausing by the fireplace, standing next to the staircase, and sitting on the kitchen counter in front of the bay windows. It was overflowing with light, so full of life.

But now the energy has turned heavy. She can see the vibrancy of the house literally withering away like dead skin peeled from fresh fruit. She feels her health being taken from her. The strength of her body feels as though it has evaporated. Her eyelids lower like a person with an internal illness. Only she doesn't feel sick, just very tired and very weak. Zoe has gone through many periods of feeling scattered and fragmented, feeling divided within herself, but this time isn't like any before, which is crazy considering she is the strongest she's ever been.

She lies in her bed, fully dressed and wrapped in the comforter. She doesn't even bother switching off the lights; this has become a normal routine. She feels like something between the walls of the house is sucking everything she has out of her. Staring at the flooring, at the ceiling, at the walls, without batting an eyelash, without a doubt, she hates this place and it hates her back. Still with no symptoms indicating sickness, Zoe springs up and runs to the bathroom, vomiting stomach acid. She's only thrown up three times in her life when no liquor was involved: when Kingston murdered Goldie and during her two pregnancies. Weeping above the greenish yellow slime in the toilet, a mirror of herself being eaten inside out, she somehow gathers the strength to go on with her day.

'I cannot stay here much longer. I've got to get out of this place,' she thinks.

Leaving to drop the kids off at school, slightly hunched over, she is too queasy and unbalanced to stand up straight. Over the years, Zoe has trained herself not to even look in the direction of that woman's house. But on this day, as the kids race to the car, Zoe freezes at the sight of those steep, slanted wooden stairs, following them with her eyes as they lead her to the woman's front door. Like a magnet, something pulls her attention over to a window and there she stands with her curtains pinned to the side, staring back at her. The old woman's eyes are puffed like a beetle's, with brittle, matted gray plaits pointed in all angles over her head. Like a proud, victorious animal watching its prey stagger to its death, she looks down at Zoe.

Just like there's light and darkness, positive and negative, heaven and hell, the Messiah and Satan, at that very moment, Zoe knows in her heart and in her head, "This woman has done something to me."

Screened in a dispiriting gray ash of defeat, Zoe begins to plan before everything is taken away, scouting for a place far from the land which has tried to ruin her life with grief. She can actually see the city leaching the color from her skin. She finds a beautiful suburb in Texas, over a thousand miles away. Listed as one of the top five best places to live in the United States, crime rating practically at zero percent, it is a very diverse, middle-to-upper-class neighborhood. School test scores are high, with over a ninety percent graduation rate.

Like enslaved Africans who have been deprived of their beliefs and their directions, Zoe feels torn from all, and injected with despair and confusion. Without a second thought, she shuts everything down—both businesses and her home—the only life she and her kids have ever known. While feeling rejected and shoved into a corner, there is a part of her that is happily willing to leave, to move over a thousand miles away. Moving away from all she's tried to bury and from the tornadoed relationship she and Vinny have created.

~ Twenty-Six ~

As a woman feeling free of every spell cast upon her, she begins to reshape her identity. Working as an independent signing agent for lenders and borrowers, experiencing only a twenty-minute to two-hour nip into her clients' lives then never having to see them again, it is such a relief to have work that isn't spilling over into her personal life. Now there's time for relaxing, taking long walks, going into deep meditations, allowing herself to enter herself, constantly reflecting on what brought her into this dimension.

She stumbles across a charming park, as enchanting as a magical island. She takes the kids there and they run around playing, blowing long bubbles, jumping on and off the play land, and swinging on the swings as high as they will go. There is a huge orange blossom tree with draping limbs weighed down by greenery and gorgeous white flowers, metaphysically drawing Zoe to it the moment she lays eyes on it. She sits next to it or lies across a blanket in front of it, praying and inhaling the peace, knowing most people find her actions impulsive, but her spirit says it is a large part of her own private destiny. She realizes another part of her healing process has begun, and without reference or explanation, she has to go on this journey; the unseen depends on it.

They travel back north for the Fourth of July to spend the holiday with family. The kids are excited to see everyone, and since it is summer break (and with a little coercing), they want to stay for a few extra weeks. Leaving her babies behind, Zoe returns home.

The first morning, Zoe wakes up to a house absent of sound—no chattering, no cartoons coming from the living room, no tiny feet padding against this wooden flooring. She goes to work that day without eating. Returning in the evening to a home with no kids, there's no reason to cook and still her body hasn't signaled for food.

Seventy-two hours later, Zoe recognizes how drastic her schedule has changed since she's been back home apart from her kids, and she regrets letting them stay. The decision was hers, there's no one else to blame, so unfortunately, she has to deal with it. And she doesn't deal with it well. She hasn't realized how much of her motivating force is driven by the presence of her children. Perhaps it is too soon to have visited their loved ones. Perhaps it would've been wiser to have kept the kids by her side. Alone, the fear begins to set in.

"You're nothing but a self-saboteur. You're passive and weak."

The fact that she believes herself to be running, it's easy to believe everything else the enemy tells her. By the end of that second week, she packs all that fits in her car, puts the rest in storage, and drives twenty hours straight—straight back to her babies and straight back to the city she hates. Zoe quickly finds a suitable community in a rural area about twenty-five miles outside town.

Carefully searching for employment, she only considers jobs which will allow her to exercise her passion of helping people and something flexible that won't undermine her personal goals. Chris calls, informing Zoe of a court-appointed service for juveniles looking to hire providers. (Zoe and Chris met through mutual friends, their personalities an instant match. Over the years, they've become a support system for each other.)

After researching the program, she falls in love with its mission to assist in rebuilding the youth and reuniting families. The job is perfect. It is exactly what she wants to do and it's the platform she needs to network and to receive additional training for the organization she's planning to create in the near future. Letting this opportunity pass her by isn't an option. She uses the remainder of that day and night tweaking her resume and submits it to the Youth Development Program the next morning. She submerges all her energy into acing that interview, spending every day studying and preparing. It pays off. She's hired on the spot.

There's nothing like being passionate about what you do to earn a living. It makes a difficult job easy to manage and you aren't worn out at the end of the day. At the break of dawn, your eyes pop open bright and wide, eager to tackle any task the day might bring. Zoe has a natural gift to connect and knock down barriers with her clients and their caregivers. Her personal experiences amplify weaponry to effectively approach different situations.

The majority of the children have been pounced on by the world in one way or another for so long that the abuse and the neglect are so expected the children laugh and crack jokes about it. Although it doesn't feel right, they accept it as normal for survival reasons, and many of them have no clue where their attitude stems from. When asked, they repeat all the names people have called them.

I'm just bad.

I'm ADD.

I'm ADHD.

I have an anger disorder.

I'm just like my mother.

I'm fast.

I'm a hustler.

I'm just like my father.

It makes it more magical, as well as causes some teary-eyed moments, when witnessing the walls they've built up come tumbling down. It is what motivates her, it is what she loves about the job, watching the injured spirits of these young people rise up from such hopeless pits.

Zoe realizes she has been gaining strength from their achievements and they help rebuild her self-confidence. She's being pieced back together by their ability to see the inner her. She can openly expose that person in her heart who's been wanting so badly to be released, without fearing someone trying to dominate her. These children in need don't see her as an object. They see her passion, perceive her wisdom, and receive her guidance. The light in their faces is what makes her feel successful.

✻

"Just like them, family members and the people closest to me have called me names. Something in my soul said, "Don't listen to them", but it had stuck in my mind because that's what they'd labeled me. They viewed a child, a person, through an eye other than love and they saw me as rebellious, disrespectful, promiscuous, less than, a dropout, a prostitute."

Dr. Brooks adjusts her glasses and says, "You know Zoe," then she pauses, taking a deep breath before continuing. "Sometimes when people are hurting, they say hurtful things."

Zoe quickly responds as if she's been waiting to release her feelings. "Those harsh words almost made me forget the pain I'd endured. The way and the how the kids end up in these places and these situations, then being made to believe they chose this route because they were born sick children. I know exactly what that feels like! If it had not been for my spirit constantly showing me the black shadows hanging above my abusers, I would have believed wholeheartedly my identity to be what they'd tagged me. It wasn't until I started working with Michelle that I received more clarity, enabling me to reach a different level in my own healing process."

From an emotional perspective, Zoe's twenties were garbage, constantly in reformation, while establishing herself as a professional and business woman. She was fighting daily to reconstruct herself and her outlook of the world. Some of the people whose paths she crossed saw a resilient woman, a strong woman destined to be an entrepreneur, but in Zoe's eyes, she was in recovery, figuring out ways to rehabilitate herself because of the silent thunderstorm within her and the fact that she didn't trust anyone else's help.

☙❁❧

The early-evening air on this September day is lukewarm with a mild breeze. As she steps out her car, she slides her arms into her suit jacket, then latches on to the handle of her briefcase. Walking toward the doors of a group home for teenage girls, she is enthused and curious about meeting her new client for the first time. Prior to the initial meeting, providers are given a case file which includes all known information as well as the client's needs and goals. To avoid approaching the situation with preconceived opinions, Zoe never reads the client's history until after establishing some form of a relationship.

When she enters the facility, she's greeted by the owner with a sarcastic smirk, ready for a tell-all gossip party. Zoe knows her kind from a mile away, so she gives her no room to spark a conversation.

"If it's all right, I would like to have a brief one-on-one with Michelle. We'll go over her paperwork, and once we finish up, could you rejoin us so we can schedule a day for me to meet with her out in the community?"

Michelle lifelessly strolls into the conference room and sits down in the chair across from Zoe. When asked how she's doing, she replies fine and slumps forward, staring down at her lap. So little and frail, if dealt a different hand, she'd still be enjoying the cartoon channel. Just as easily as you can tell she's a young girl, you can tell something forced her into adulthood. Quickly observing the many delicate layers, Zoe back-pedals her thoughts, preparing herself because she senses cracking her shell is going to require plenty of patience.

Zoe begins asking her questions for no other reason than to get her to somewhat engage, or at the very least, get a little eye contact. It isn't until Zoe is leaving that Michelle finally looks her square in the face. There's pure *pain in her eyes. She looks like a lost orphan. The way Zoe's heart sinks has never happened before. Zoe is* startled with disbelief. It's as if she's looking at herself. Her instincts wail on the inside to wrap her arms around the little girl and vow to do everything she can to help her.

She puts one hand on Michelle's shoulder and says, "I know I may not look like it, but I've been in some extremely dark places and I need you to believe me: This will only last for a moment. It will pass. One day you're going to look up and you'll be in a place that will be a lot less painful."

Tears are in both of their eyes as Zoe reassures her she'll stand by her side. The tears begin to roll down Michelle's cheeks. The urge to hug her becomes harder to restrain. She knows it's important not to because a main part of the program is to teach boundaries for their safety and for the safety of others. She doesn't expect Michelle to lay her head on her collarbone, but there's no way Zoe is going to shrug her off. She pats her back while she empties out what seems to be an accumulation over many years.

It is a long ride home. No music, just driving through the midnight blue, thinking nonstop about her client who she didn't know existed until two hours ago. Zoe has worked with many children, sympathizing with each one of them because they have all experienced more than their fair share of adversity. But to not provide a disservice, you can't allow your emotions to be engulfed by the client's issues. The only way to effectively help them is to slightly detach yourself, keeping a clear and relaxed mind so you can remain grounded. Zoe understands the importance of being centered for the job and herself, and she has mastered it—until now.

She is unable to dismiss the similarity of Michelle's reflection and the way she cried, the same kind of silent cry that flowed from Zoe when her small body couldn't take any more. Still with no knowledge of what the State has documented, she knows without a doubt this kid has been abused, most likely in more ways than one, and has felt forced to deal with the abuse all alone. Being trained to cry in secrecy, afraid to share the pain, that's how a child learns to cry through a closed mouth—silently, not making a sound.

Other clients come and go, but Michelle stays and Zoe spends the next couple of years assisting her in recovering from the aftermath of her suffering. Throughout their journey, Zoe somehow pushes aside the reality that she too has endured trauma just as flabbergasting. They both have been tortured in the same way, and just like Zoe, the majority of Michelle's afflictions have come from the nearly-global verdict that she chose this life and is the cause of her own pain.

A lot of people she works cases with randomly ask her the most-simple questions. Her belief is they are digging, trying to find where her passion stems from. She never answers their questions, always managing to smoothly redirect the conversations, because answering them will only lead to more questions.

The tension grows between Zoe and some of the other professionals assigned to Michelle's case. She is disgusted by the bureau worker grossly fighting to keep the little girl in group homes and residential facilities, arguing, "She needs to remain in a secure placement because she's a danger to herself." Then, when the client isn't around, with a dry social remark, she'll say things like, "The apple doesn't fall far from the tree," or "We can't save them all." These commentaries are too much for Zoe's heart and too much for her to have enough self-control not to strike her eyes upside the bureau worker's head.

The division is no secret. They always take seats at opposite ends of the table, both sides displaying disbelief on their faces, regarding one another's intense responses, being dissectors and studying every word spoken. Zoe isn't sure if it's a black-and-white or a tax-bracket issue. Whatever the situation is, the encounters with the bureau worker always leave Zoe outraged at the corruption of power and the willful ignorance of the female and child's vulnerabilities.

Vinny frequently comes around. They try with all their might to don the masks and cover their sense of loss, hiding behind the billboard that reads, "We have kids together. Everyone needs to respect our co-parenting." The truth is, they have a cynical bond that can't be broken. It isn't about the kids; they've become co-dependent on each other, like protective animals, detecting when something is wrong. They have no detailed knowledge of what is actually going on in their separate lives, yet they can powerfully sense troublesome obstacles or the hollowing shift in one another's spirits.

The relationship has changed, and with the absence of steady sex, they begin to build a different foundation, and when they sense each other's inner screams of things being rough, these were the moments the tender looks resurface. As natural partners, they are quick to embrace and to affirm security, then try not to speak about it, as if their efforts to overcome the weakness of their flesh might be jeopardized.

Through this part of their separation, they learn how much love, how much jealousy, how much support is based on sex, and how much sex is based on intercourse. Discovering sensual feelings from being quiet together, playing games with their kids, watching movies, and enjoying a tasteful meal, Zoe does not comprehend until years later that the building blocks they use to build this new foundation is made of a concrete much stronger than copulation.

~ Twenty-Seven ~

Zoe walks through a set of French doors, stepping on to a wooden heated deck, a plush white robe touching the heels of her feet. Grabbing hold of the double-breasted section, she slowly peels it off her back, laying it on top of a small round glass table and revealing a shiny black bathing suit with queen slits around the chest area. The rising warmth keeps her unbothered by the freezing temperatures as she submerges her body in the hot tub full of high-powered jets beating against her from every angle as if she is trapped inside a washing machine. The steam billows against the cold air creating smoke, and it swells and swirls and dances above Zoe's head.

She can't hear anything other than the bubbling sound from the water. She relaxes the back of her head on the granite stone etching the edge of the hot tub, off in the back country enjoying the glorious scenery in Aspen. A distant view shows gigantic trees and mountain slopes and cliffs that are over six thousand feet high, all coated with a thick layer of snow. As far as she can see, there are untouched mountains with powder sparkling, and she knows her dreams have come true. It all belongs to her and she isn't worried about anything. Suddenly, the Northern lights screen the sky. Zoe inhales with astonishment at the beautiful glow.

In that very second, a large masculine hand cuffs the curve of her right shoulder. As she begins to turn, she glances at his wedding band. In her heart, she knows it is her husband. Spinning around to meet his eyes, she looks upon their almond-colored log home, formed in the shape of a horseshoe, with a yellow incandescence shining through the many uncurtained glass windows. She knows once their faces are aligned, something amazing is going to happen. The phone rings. She wants to ignore it, but it won't stop ringing, so she tries to push the 'end' button before the caller ruins their moment. She begins to smile; it is finally silent again.

"Hello? Can you hear me?"

"Huh?" she responds, extremely confused.

"I'm sorry, is this Zoe?" Her eyes pop wide open and she clears her throat. "What? Who is this?"

"I didn't mean to wake you. This is Scotti. I wanted to catch you before you started your day to see if we can meet up for lunch or possibly after work. I have something important to speak with you about and I'd really like to do it in person."

By seven-fifteen, she is dressed, sitting at the dining room table, checking her emails over a cinnamon raisin bagel and a fresh brewed cup of coffee. As she waits for her children to finish getting ready for school, she finds her concentration to be scattered, so she hooks the leash on the dog's collar and stands outside until the little ones came running out.

The entire morning goes smoothly. Around twelve-thirty, Zoe arrives at the restaurant to meet Scotti. She can't imagine what he wants to talk about. Every now and again, they bump into one another, but it is nowhere near often and they only keep enough in contact to know how to connect with each other if they need to. Just as hungry as she is curious, she flies in the doors, immediately spotting him at a corner booth with his cell phone pasted to his ear. He rises as she approaches the table and greets her with a long, warm hug.

"You really look great, Zoe. More so than that, you look like life's been treating you well."

"Thank you, and you're looking pretty good yourself."

They smile at each other and he kisses her on the cheek. After settling down, they catch each other up on their personal lives as they wait for the waitress to bring out their food. Once the meals are spread over the table and they have started satisfying their bellies, Zoe asks, "Is everything okay? It just seemed like something was wrong when you called me this morning."

With an uncomfortable smirk, he says, "Yeah . . . um . . . I felt bad for waking you up. It sounded like you were underneath the bed." They let out a short laugh.

"Yes," she nods, "I was sleeping good."

There is a look of hesitation, a change-of-mind expression in the medium of their words. She becomes slightly concerned in the awkward silence and his actions cause her to hesitate. Scotti gently lays down his fork and swallows the food in his mouth like his throat has shrunk.

He looks toward the window, staring at the cars as they drive by.

"Scotti, whatever it is, you can tell me."

His voice is low and saddened. "I just . . . sort of feel like I'm betraying my friend. I know he has some issues, but we grew up together and I've got a lot of love for him. But I really care about you too, and the fact is, what Kingston did was just so wrong . . . Sometimes I wish I had done something."

Cocking her head to the side with a blank stare directed at the center of his face, she holds a contorted little smile to keep from looking angry.

"I don't know if you heard or not that Kingston is locked up."

Struggling to keep her attitude in check, her lips tighten into a straight line, and in a firm voice, she replies, "I know nothing about him, and whatever is going on in his life has nothing to do with me."

"Zoe, I'm so sorry. The last thing I want is to upset you. This whole situation has been weighing on me . . ."

"Please just get to the point."

"Well . . . um . . . He's being indicted by the Feds on fourteen counts of sex trafficking children."

Zoe tries as hard as she can to block his words from entering her ears, but still they slither their way in.

"He's taking a plea agreement, so there won't be a trial. His sentencing hearing is next month, and the victims and their families will be able to speak. I feel like you should tell your story. If you don't want to take the stand, you should consider sharing your experiences with the district attorney."

There are so many emotions flipping through her body that it holds her tears at bay. She doesn't know how she can feel all these things at once, but she does.

"I was angry at my lack of courage. Had I spoken all those years ago, there would have been no other victims."

Zoe is disgusted at the sound of Kingston's name and nauseated by what she knows those other kids must have gone through because she'd experienced it firsthand. More than that and as selfish as it may have been, she is outraged at Scotti for inconsiderately digging up what she's worked so hard to bury. Zoe battles with pushing away the thoughts by mildly shaking her head, hoping to distract her mind, but it doesn't work. The thoughts keep coming as Scotti sits quietly studying her.

Memories start flooding back, flashes of visions Zoe has totally forgotten. She stands up and mumbles, "I have to go back to work now."

Scotti stands up and steps toward her. It takes everything in her not to start punching him. The sight of his face, the sound of his voice is like nails scraping across a chalkboard. She prays for him not to touch her, and when he hugs her goodbye, she feels even more violated. As he watches her wend her way through the restaurant, she manages to hold her composure until she gets in the car, bowing her head over the steering wheel as the restraint fails.

The remainder of Zoe's work day isn't good or bad; all her feelings are deadened. Driving home, Scotti's words play in her mind for the umpteenth time, and she convinces herself that the only thing bothering her is Scotti and his irritating voice. When she gets home, she is exhausted, dropping down across the center of her bed, just wanting to go to sleep, but she can't stop reviewing the events of her day: the early-morning random phone call, the look on Scotti's face, the words spoken, and all the things she should've said.

For the sudden dislike she has developed for him over the past six hours, Zoe subconsciously remembers some of the many warmhearted gestures Scotti made toward her, starting from the first day they met. But it is all too painful, and as an award-winning marathon runner of the mind, she begins forcing herself to sleep, sprinting from her thoughts. As she drifts off, her internal alarm is ringing a warning bell. Something tells her not to ignore it; however, she rolls over, pulling the blanket up, swiftly rejecting all feelings. Zoe tosses the whole night, falling into one troublesome dream after another.

She restlessly lies in bed the next morning, recalling parts of the dreams. Jackson and Vinny and Kingston were all in it, and there was a voice with no face, but it sounded exactly like Scotti's voice arguing, saying, "Zoe, you need to speak up. How can you be so selfish? How can you turn your back?" Jackson was lying in pure darkness, and all she could see was his eyes and teeth. He was squeezing her hand, pleading to be saved, saying, "I don't want to die. What about my baby? Zoe, help me. Please do something."

Springing to her feet, she runs to the sink, splashing water on her face, hoping for relief. After all these years of no panic attacks, now, out of the blue, it is happening again. Heart racing, short of breath, perspiration forming over her entire body, there's no more room to stuff any more memories. They begin to erupt. Memories of being verbally ripped to shreds, being twelve years old, playing the piano, a brown-and-gold casket disappearing into the ground, being beaten, sitting in the orchestra playing the violin, a strange man drooling over a tiny body, Vinny and her wrapping the brokenness between their arms.

Zoe slides down to the bathroom floor, clutching her chest. She starts coaching herself out loud to cease the thoughts, slowly repeating, "Okay, okay, okay," until her breathing is regulated.

❧✹❧

"Privately, I started researching Kingston's case, and privately, I was at the center of it. Every morning, every day, every night I found a free second, I searched through his court case. There were so many questions. I wanted to know how many more kids had he hurt and I wondered how many were remaining silent like me. I wanted to know who was the bold person who had courageously screamed out for help to stop this demon from snatching up more young girls with damaged souls. I wondered if he had done the same things to them he had done to me, or if, by chance over the years, the universe might have made him a little nicer.

"I researched his lawyer. I needed to know who was defending him and how did a so-called sane person present a compelling argument for such a wicked man. I was sickened to my stomach behind each motion Kingston's lawyer had filed to exclude evidence because he believed it would put his client at risk of an unfair hearing. I also researched all the legal parties involved on the prosecution team. The United States Attorney James L. Santelle, the Assistant United States Attorneys Melvin K. Washington and Joseph R. Wall, as well as the special agents with the Federal Bureau of Investigation. I questioned the concern and motive of each of them because I had never been able to get out my mind that moment I'd thought the police force was about to save me from Kingston, but then I'd found out they had a different agenda that was more important than the life of a random little girl from the inner city.

"I obtained the phone numbers to all their offices and saved each of them under their names in my contact list. Sometimes I'd call them anonymously, but as soon as someone would pick up, I'd get scared and hang up. I just didn't have the guts to talk and I didn't want to be put on the spot. There were some things I could never repeat—not ever—not under any circumstances. I wasn't seeking revenge for myself. I didn't even feel the hatred I'd once felt. I just knew he was sick, the kind of sick only God can heal, but God gives free will and I didn't believe he had the willingness to seek salvation.

"I couldn't decide what his destination should be—prison or a mental institution—because I was no judge. However, I did think he needed to go to a special place that only kept people like him—a place with no bridges, no roads, keeping them secluded from ever having access to children for the remainder of their lives. To abuse a child in such a way is worse than murdering their victims. I was sure most family members of the deceased would disagree. But those family members, those prosecutors, those judges, and those defense attorneys couldn't fathom how many times a child victimized by this crime dies throughout the duration of their lifetime."

The following was not written by the author of *Smoking Out the Shadows*. Documentation was obtained by a third party and the documents were gathered from the United States District Court files. The indictment packet is too large and most things are not necessary to disclose. Only a few selected paragraphs from the sentencing memorandum which was submitted by Mr. X, who is the attorney for Mr. Z, aka Kingston, are disclosed here. It reads:

UNITED STATES OF AMERICA, Plaintiff,

v.

Case No. #Y, Defendant.

SENTENCING MEMORANDUM

In the case of Mr. Z, a sentence of 25 years of imprisonment, with a lifetime of extended supervision, is sufficient but not greater than necessary to meet the requirements of §3553(2).

Case Procedural History and Status

Mr. Z was charged in a fourteen count Third Superseding indictment with one count of Conspiracy to Sex Traffic in Children; two counts of Sex Trafficking of a Child by Use of Force, Fraud or Coercion; four counts of Transporting a Child to Engage in Prostitution; four counts of Sex Trafficking of a Child; one count of Transportation for Purposes of Prostitution; and two counts of Production of Child Pornography.

A presentence investigation was conducted by the United States Probation Office, and the presentence writer determined that the applicable total offense level, including a three-level reduction for acceptance of responsibility, is 40 years old. With a criminal history category of III, the advisory guideline imprisonment range in Mr. Z's case is 360 months to life imprisonment. Neither the Government nor Mr. Z dispute this is the correct advisory sentencing guidelines range in this case. 25 years of imprisonment is sufficient, but not greater than necessary to meet the requirements of 18 U.S.C. §3553(2) in the case of #.

With regard to the requirement of §3553(2) that the sentence should reflect the seriousness of the offense, there is no denying that child sex trafficking is a terrible crime, and calls for imposition of a lengthy prison sentence. However, it is equally undeniable that a twenty-five-year sentence is an extraordinarily harsh punishment. Twenty-five years is such a large part of one's life to lose that it is difficult to fathom the regret and despair an inmate with such a sentence must suffer. Few people would take the position that twenty-five years is not a severe punishment for any human being—and a warning to others who might otherwise commit similar types of crimes.

A mitigating factor in the case of Mr. Z's specific crime, it must be noted, is that the victims in this case were not young children, but were in fact close to becoming legally adults. While Mr. Z profited from his crime, and is paying the price, it cannot be said about the victims that they are the most vulnerable people in society—our babies and young children. Unfortunately, because of the nature of the charges in this case—child sex trafficking—this mitigating factor must be recognized in Mr. Z's defense. Mr. Z is deeply remorseful for his crimes, and struggles every day to understand how he allowed himself to do what he did. To the Court he wrote: "I can't even explain why I played any part of what I did. I give it thought every single day and I even sicken myself."

Because this is a sex-related case, it is significant that there was no indication Mr. Z has a deviant sexual interest which might drive him to reoffend in the future by sexually assaulting another person. Mr. Z has never been arrested for any type of sexual misconduct, and there is nothing to indicate he has ever behaved in a sexually inappropriate manner in the past. Mr. Z is not an incorrigible sex offender, for example, with an abnormal and diagnosable sexual interest in young children, which may or may not be treatable with psychiatric care or counseling. Fortunately for Mr. Z, he has a lower risk of offending in the future than a person with those types of mental health issues, and deviant sexual desires.

By all appearances, these crimes of Mr. Z's seem to be mostly motivated by a desire to make money, along with a complete failure to understand the devastation sexual offenses can have on the victims, and their families. Mr. Z struggles to understand his own actions and decisions, but it may be relevant that he was a victim of sexual abuse himself, as a child. Also, Mr. Z never had a strong, positive male role model in his life.

Mr. Z's insights into his crimes, and his remorse, largely motivated his acceptance of responsibility in this case. Even though he is faced with an advisory guidelines range at the top of the scale, where other defendants might think they've got nothing to lose and, as such, roll the dice with trial, Mr. Z did not put the Government to its burden of proof. But even more significant in his decision to plead guilty was his desire to spare the victims and their family members, and his own family, from the embarrassment and pain of a trial. A trial of this case would have lasted weeks, been riddled with sordid and embarrassing testimony, eaten up the valuable and limited time of the Court, and cost the taxpayers many thousands of dollars. As such, Mr. Z's decision to accept responsibility for his crimes will have a higher-than-average and very tangible value to the courts, the taxpayers, the government, and most of all, to the victims in this case. In any event, Mr. Z has accepted responsibility in a genuine and profound way, and asks the Court to take this into account when fashioning a reasonable sentence for him.

Conclusion

For these reasons, the defendant, Mr. Z, by his attorney, Mr. X, asks the Court to impose a sentence of twenty-five years.

☙✸❧

Zoe can't help wondering, what would be the protocol if a police officer found their little girl in the hands of an old man? What would be the words they used to describe their daughter after discovering the ways a predator had disturbed her body? She remembers seeing the breaking news on several missing child cases. Each time, the world froze as the media gave detailed coverage of how the child escaped or was rescued. The chief of police and other community activist would rally together around a podium and you could tell they were going to make sure that sick, demonic, menacing child molester would never again see the light of day. They'd speak about the "abduction" and the great efforts they would be putting forth to assist the victims during the healing process. It is such a huge difference in the actions and the vocabulary used when a black kid is taken standing in front of their house or walking home from a bus stop.

The injustice by society eats away at another area of her belief system, breeding a resentment and distrust for the white culture. A part of her grows more determined to prove to "them" that she and her "people" possess an utmost power to rise up above all oppression even without being coddled. Another part of her begins to scorn at the artificialness, the immorality that's vanquishing and continually substantiating this to be white America. But there is another part of her that's being drenched in memories, trapping her in an undecodable illusion, which once again disjoints her from the world.

Zoe's thoughts are loud. She's being hunted, and she starts to move faster and to engage in things of no interest, basically running as though she can surpass them. Everything Zoe tries fails. It's like the fourteen years she has between Kingston and the day Scotti took her to lunch has evaporated. The rational side of her appears to be in control, and she finds it hard to keep the groaning inside from leaking out.

'Who are you trying to fool? You're weak and everybody knows it. It's all your fault. Everything that happened to you, you deserved it.'

She gets angry for allowing the negativity and the unchecked memories access to her mind. She can't understand how this is happening all over again to her. She was confident she'd mastered her self-management steps. Now, instead of managing, she wishes she'd known how to resolve those problems as they occurred rather than carrying them within her all this time.

Trapped in a net no one can pluck her free from, she is filled with fear as one wave after another crashes into her. It feels like a nuclear bomb has detonated and holes are being eaten through her flesh as her bones deteriorate. She's drowning in the depths of a jet-black sea with no way to stay afloat. She's become accustomed to the luxury of turning to her religion as a source of relief and inspiration, but the comfort has been fading. The need for more has fallen into a demand, and she looks up and finds herself religiously bankrupt. Then disturbance unfolds throughout her world.

At night, Zoe lies in bed listening, concentrating, for any noise alluding to an intruder. Then randomly, the stimulation takes over. She jumps up, peeking into every room, making sure the doors are all bolted, then looking out the windows for any suspicious activities. Her eyes change from brown to black, casting back the horrifying scenes playing in her head. She can no longer utilize the invisible walls and the weapons she's once used; they silently fall.

Working for the Youth Development Program use to be a reliable diversion. Now, if a coworker or client looks at her funny or says something that might have been innocent, her personal issues will impose on the rest of her work day.

While Zoe is crumbling, Michelle appears to be getting stronger, or maybe a better description for her is deadened—deadened toward the whole system. The State places her in another group home with a list of rules and restrictions. The bottom line is she isn't permitted to leave the facility except for school or with a case worker. The bureau worker uses her going to visit her family as an incentive, so she goes to school and clowns until she gets suspended. Then they return to the round table, trying to figure out another treatment plan. For what, when the final plan is always something that will never be effective?

In the meantime, Michelle is mentally weighing out the pros and cons, giving the bare minimum of cooperation because she feels like she is being treated like a criminal and she has nothing to lose. Without a hint of any facial expression, just a locked-in stare at the mid-air, she speaks only when spoken to, responding with the shortest answer possible to the rawness in the bureau worker's voice as if she is baiting Michelle to give a more-heated response.

"Clearly, you're taking this as a joke. We'll be scheduling another meeting for next month, and don't forget you've now lost your pass to spend the weekend with your family. If you still decide to leave, I've told the group home to notify the police so a detainer can be placed on you." She cocks her ice-cold blue eyes upside the child's head, popping a sarcastic smirk across her lips, like, "Now what?"

For a moment, Michelle's defenses are weakened, and you can see a glimpse of the pain, although the stand she chooses to take is to remain disconnected. Clearly, she's tussling with losing face as her lips start to tremble, gaining some control by tucking them in against her teeth. Her eyes start to well up with tears. At this point, all Michelle can hold on to is the refusal to participate. Abruptly rising to her feet, she walks away without looking at any of them.

The energy ricochets throughout Zoe's entire body, demanding to be discharged, fueled by the wickedness being fatally drizzled into the veins of children, into the woman who was created to bear fruit and to nurture, and into the races of color who are beating against the metal bars of survival and acceptance.

In a chilling, vehement tone, Zoe floors the room when she blurts out, "How many times has your child acted out and the consequence you saw fit was for them not to be allowed into their own home? What kind of punishment is that?"

They frown at each other and it takes everything in Zoe not to punch her. If it wasn't for the look on the bureau worker's face, who seems to be both expecting and begging her to do it, she might have lost all self-control. The bureau worker gives the room a dismissive smile. It takes great efforts for Zoe to end the meeting as a professional, with a growing itch of dislike for this person that spread over her like poison ivy. The nastiness inside the bureau worker's spirit proudly steps into the light, leaving itself unveiled and the phoniness is exposed as the manipulative, spiteful, evil serpentine boldly steps in front of everybody.

Knowing this isn't even her worst side, Zoe bites her tongue as she walks off to find Michelle. She finds her sitting on the edge of a twin-size bed, her face listless. She isn't supposed to touch her—it is considered unethical—but if there is no one there to embrace a victim, how can they learn to embrace themselves? With no thought, as if it was her own child, she puts her arm around her, sitting beside her for about five minutes beneath a heavy silence.

"I think some fresh air would be good right now," Zoe suggests.

They ride at a moderate speed, listening to soft music, both lost in their own heads. Stopping for a light at the intersection, she doesn't know which way to turn.

"Is there somewhere you wanna go?"

"I really don't want to be around a lot of people."

"Okay."

Zoe gives a nod of agreement and heads east toward her favorite spot. It is where she always goes whenever she feels confused or under attack, and in need of God to work a miracle. While en route, they stop by a small coffee shop, picking up two large cappuccinos. Shortly after, they are standing out on the pier, watching the reckless waves slam against the shore, enjoying the comfort from the hotness of their drinks.

Michelle is the first to walk off, taking a seat on top of a wall formed with huge rocks. Zoe follows and sits on the rock next to her. She still hasn't gotten all the details of Michelle's past. She learns from her own experiences that it is best to just let people discuss what they want, when they want. But sometimes, she looks at Michelle and wishes she knew more, then she kills that thought because she knows people look at her the same way.

Michelle stares, frowning down at the rocks and sand as if what she's lost might be scattered over the gravel. Zoe can see her slipping away, sliding beneath the welcoming pain that is waiting patiently in the center of her chest. Her face turns red. She tilts her head up toward the sky and a river of tears stream from her eyes. The hardened shell takes flight, leaving this little girl all alone, naked with no protection. Grace breaks through this cryptic minute of joined distrust, uncertainty, and skepticism. The plug is removed and fifteen years of things that have been stuffed inside Michelle come flooding forth.

She speaks about the flickering flashes and the moments in which it happens, how it activates great fear. The morning she was awakened and realized she'd been stripped of both her mother and father, and they kept telling her, "Baby, we love you, and if we could be there, we would." But what she heard the people around her saying was, "She was abandoned." It really didn't matter how it had happened because the truth is, somehow, her whole family disappeared. She talks about the times she's willingly given herself away to distract her mind from the pain; the times she didn't want to, but her no's were ignored; how she'd felt to be sold; and what she truly thought of herself.

☙✹❧

Practically paralyzed with depletion as her limbs slightly start floating and the lower part of her face submerges under the bathwater, the details of Zoe's day are replayed. Suddenly, a feeling springs free of its grave, a feeling that she has been mourning her own death ever since Scotti brought Kingston back to life. Her resistance has failed even against the most-microscopic things—someone cuts her off on the road, or her steak isn't prepared properly, or a person is using more words than she thinks they should and she just wants them to hurry up and get to the point—and somehow it diminishes her to an adolescent state. The person she was forty-five days ago just flat-out doesn't exist any more.

Ever since she can remember, there were blocks of time where she's drawn blanks. Although she can't see a thing, there's a constant sense that something is lounging in the darkness, not threatening her or looking pathetic, just quietly sitting there as a guard saying, "Do not enter." She knows it once had to be some kind of clear image, but it has evolved into something much darker than a shadow, and even when summoned, it won't appear. These black blocks only seem scary when her thoughts get too close to discerning the image, so she's grown accustomed to moving around them.

That night, Zoe lights the candles on her dresser and nightstand, and lies meditating, knowing it will be one of those sleepless nights. She doesn't even bother trying to close her eyes. Tucked between the sheets in the recess of her life, out of the blue, a memory springs from nowhere.

One evening, she and Kingston went to meet a few of his guy friends at a restaurant. She'd just gotten her hair done and they were all dressed up. For some reason, it seemed like they were celebrating something, and everyone was talking and laughing. She was included in the conversations and felt totally comfortable. His close friends were really nice people. They were normal people with good jobs and continuing their education, speaking on intelligent topics. Zoe was always so happy when they came around and they made their fondness of her no secret. Kingston's face would always fill with jealousy.

When they finished dinner and everyone began to go their separate ways, Scotti asked Kingston to drop him off at his car. Kingston said no—Zoe believe he just had an attitude because she'd received too much attention—but Scotti wasn't hearing it. He insisted as he followed them through the parking lot. Zoe was walking between the two of them and Scotti asked her if she'd enjoyed her meal. They started discussing the food and the service, and Kingston began to walk a few steps ahead of them.

Neither one of them saw it coming. Zoe could tell Scotti was just as shocked as she was. One second, her face was freezing. The next second, her face was burning. By the third second, her face was numb. She squatted down, burying herself in her hands. That's when she realized she'd been hit with a slab of snow held together by chunks of ice.

Completely on impulse, Scotti yelled out, "WHAT THE HELL IS WRONG WITH YOU?!"

He too squatted down, peeling back her hands, and began to wipe the slush from her face and hair. They silently bowed forward, closing their eyes as their heads touched, and for a minute, everything paused. Inside the car, there was an extreme awkwardness vibing off each of them, total silence, until Scotti said, "There's been a change of plans. I'm gonna have my people pick me up from your apartment."

That next morning, Zoe went to use the bathroom and saw that Scotti hadn't left; he was sleeping on the couch. She looked a little longer than she should have and she was secretly ashamed of the uncontrolled smile. She could have been wrong, but she felt like his staying was a small way to protect her for the remainder of that night.

Zoe is kind of tripping that that memory from so long ago has popped in her mind, considering she'd pushed it out of her thoughts right after it happened. Maybe something wants to provide her with confirmation of her being humiliated. Or maybe, it is because she's still upset with Scotti and the universe wants to give confirmation of his kindness.

~ Twenty-Eight ~

Valentine's Day comes, and this year, Zoe hasn't had two thoughts about it. With all that has been going on, one of her favorite holidays has slipped her mind. Early that morning, Vinny texts, HAPPY VALENTINE'S DAY, SWEETS, and seals it with a smiley face. By lunchtime, they're at BW3's, eating chicken wings and waffle fries. By seven p.m., they're walking through Mayfair Mall shopping, and by nine, they're sitting down in the Marcus Cinema Theater.

It is only later in the middle of that night, when they lie tangled with their sweat mingling in salted puddles and the moonlight is bleeding through the opened blinds, that Zoe realizes, although it is still a battle, she's graduated to a higher level. His body and her body no longer possess the power to make her mind backpedal. This isn't their last time; however, it is the first time she doesn't emotionally relapse, and that is huge.

They've loved each other from the moment they laid eyes on one another, young kids with no clue what life was all about, and they've been through every chapter of their lives together. It is then she understands that these are the things she's holding onto and it isn't enough, and holding onto it, in the end, has cost them so much. Zoe knows it's primarily because they both are such devoted and affectionate people, but they have to find a way to accept that they've struck out and this friendship can't be—at least not until they learn more boundaries.

ꕥ

After attending so many different workshops, assemblies, seminars, doctor appointments, and conferences over the years for trainings and with clients for reforming purposes, Zoe is persuaded into entertaining the thought of going to talk to somebody. She's heard all kinds of experts stressing the importance of breaking the silence, and she figures since she's tried everything else, perhaps if she finds the right person, it will make a difference. At this point, the fear of completely losing her sanity is more real than ever, which humbles her into crawling to a small, private clinic, meeting with a therapist named Dr. Osman. Zoe s stunned at the doctor's looks.

'She sure didn't sound this young over the phone,' Zoe thinks, trying to keep an open mind. *'Well, maybe we'll be able to connect easier.'*

Zoe quickly observes her inexperience by the way she starts her questioning and oddly holding her eyes in a squinted position, slowly nodding her head, as if they've been in deep conversation. Perhaps it is the doctor's way of relaying comprehension or some sort of sympathy, but to Zoe, it is over the top and premature. Zoe begins to retreat. At the same time, a voice whispers in her ear, "I knew this was a stupid idea."

She must have seen the shift in Zoe and that is the reason she takes off rambling. "I believe all traumatic memories can be replaced by happy ones. You know, if you would leave whatever's bothering you in your past, you could move forward and live the life you dream of."

'I have plenty of happy memories,' Zoe thinks.

"I wish that was all it took to get rid of the bad ones, and my occasionally good dreams haven't worked either." Although she is thinking, *'Who licensed this girl?'*, she knows she needs to get some things out, so she stays, on the brink of releasing some steam. Then Dr. Osman begins talking like they're at a social hour.

"I don't mean to change the subject, but where do you get your nails done? I love that color polish."

Zoe never goes back again. She is looking forward to feeling better. Instead, she feels like for one reason or another, she won't ever be able to tell anyone everything that's going on inside her. The stirred-up concoction blends with shame, fear, anger, passion, and regret, brewing with the fact that she'll never be able to escape Kingston. And her baby is about to be a teenager and Zoe still doesn't feel strong enough to speak of Jackson; yet she feels horrible because she knows she isn't telling her a story that belongs to her, but it falls outside of language.

The deep memories are only in images and sensations, and all the other things between those things that won't shake off. Difficulty concentrating, everything is a disaster. The only ones close enough to know what is happening, other than God, are the black shadows that visit during those dreadful hours of those terrible dreams, tormenting and crouching down on her until she can't breathe. She isn't able to do anything. She feels like she's waiting on something, but who or what, she doesn't know.

꧁✸꧂

Four years or so earlier, Savannah and Zoe went out to a club for a couple of cocktails. As usual, Savannah was gliding around the place and Zoe was sitting at the end of the bar in a low-key kind of way. She didn't know who this guy was, but what he was, was plain enough for anyone with eyes to see. He was wearing a lot of colors with bold printed letters over the front of his shirt. In one hand, he held a glass of liquor and the other hand held his own bottle from which his refills came from. She deliberately avoided making eye contact, so he decided to take a seat on the stool to the left of her, attempting multiple times to spark a conversation. The music was thumping loud and he was already hazed and the stench of weed was almost louder than the club. Zoe turned her face toward him, looking as if he was less than.

He said, "Come on, Miss Lady, don't be acting like that. We don't know each other, but I've seen you quite a few times. You be at this house that's right around the corner from my house. I always wanted to speak to you, but I didn't know how to approach you. I was shocked to see you in here and I couldn't let this chance get away. I just want to introduce myself and at least find out your name."

His words made her feel some kind of way for being so rude.

"Forgive me; my name is Zoe."

She shook his hand and he jumped straight into his life's story, explaining the environment he'd been raised in on the west side of Chicago, forming him into a professional of all kinds of thuggery. and now he was in the process of transitioning to being an honorable painter. Savannah resurfaced just in time. She didn't even notice the guy as she stole Zoe away.

After that night, it seemed like every time Zoe stopped by her mother's house, this guy was driving past, waving or honking the horn. He caught her one day, sitting in her car. She was a little bothered, so she'd let the kids go in to visit with the family and she'd stayed in the car for a few moments to unwind. He pulled up alongside her, and within a couple of minutes, they'd exchanged phone numbers.

When he started calling, she'd immediately started brushing him off. At that time, overall, things were going smoothly for Zoe. The first business had been operating for a while, her and Vinny had pretty much adjusted to their new, divided three-day-a-week relationship, and she wasn't looking to have a commitment to anyone else. Plus, this guy didn't fit the profile of a man who would attract her anyway. Her feelings were no secret, so he tried buying her attention. Eventually, after not reaching second base, he faded away.

Now, Zoe is visiting her family and her mother yells into the kitchen, "ZO, SOMEBODY WANTS YOU OUTSIDE!"

She walks out the front door, and to her surprise, that guy from four years ago is standing there next to a neon-colored Tahoe truck and his outfit looks like he's been wrapped in the rainbow.

He apologizes for popping up, saying, "I didn't know how to find you and I just wanted to see your face."

She isn't sure what blows her mind more—the nerve of him to show up at her mother's door, or all those stupid colors he's wearing. At this time in Zoe's life, while she is dealing with Scotti and Kingston and all the things before and after them, it isn't safe for anyone to enter her space. She's begun to unravel and anything that's irritating, especially outside of work, catches the whips of her anger. This guy doesn't care; he is even more persistent than before. Either he thinks his money can make her love him, or having a piece of her is worth no affection. Right away, he begins making offers.

"I knew I shouldn't have come here. I had to build up a lot of courage to knock on that door. Baby, clearly, we're cut from two different cloths, but I just want to be your friend. I wanna look out for you; money is no problem. I'll give you whatever you want. Is there something you need right now?"

Along with all the other things that are already happening, his words trigger another issue, another side of Zoe that hasn't been dealt with. Her eyes slice into him and the thought, *'Oh, so you're trying to treat me like a ho?'* bursts forth. Finding what someone else may think are kind words as only a veneer, she feels that beneath the surface he is disrespecting her, and she decides to return the treatment.

"Yeah, I need twelve hundred dollars."

"For what?"

"Business."

"When?"

"Now."

"I'll have to go get it. Can we meet somewhere for lunch? I haven't eaten yet and I'll bring that with me."

In the days following, he continues paying for her company and flooding her with gifts. And she continues handling him like crap because she knows his acts are out of desperation. Yet, he patiently waits for one thing.

Zoe doesn't like any part of this guy. She shrinks from his touch; however, once that pitiful look settles in, taking residency on his face, she feels like a monster and begins to feel obligated to give him something as vital as what he thinks he's giving to her. She forces herself to be a little nicer by zeroing in on the one desire she has for him.

She tries to go with it for a while, but neither her heart or her mind is in it. Neither he or his money or any other man holds the adequate balance of sensitivity, endurance, and mental acuteness Zoe needs. They both have problems, and her way of displaying that she is the stronger of the two is by violating his masculinity. She doesn't feel respected by men, so she doesn't want a man she can respect, but one she can master, finding a small amount of sick excitement in becoming the man and assisting him into changing into the woman.

Once the disrespect is smeared across the table, Zoe finds herself consciously fighting with this guy she knows she can never love, dumping her frustration and wrath on him. She is enmeshed in a scrimmage with this guy only because he's in her space along with all the real things she's actually angry about, that she's sick of battling, so she chooses to battle with him:

The vision of her inaction in the presence of her mother's long-suffering caused by the father she uncontrollably ached for. The vision of the last time she allowed her family to suck her into their mess, which resulted in a physical altercation with her cousin's mother. She'd loved her cousin's mother more than she loved half the people she shared the same bloodline with. A couple of months after the altercation, she'd died. Zoe never had the chance to apologize, so she'd grieved with no one by her side. Parking far away from the crowd, she'd watched from the driver's seat as they lowered her final bed into the ground.

The vision of many events turning the pure love between her and Vinny into total recklessness. The vision of Jackson's face in every way that her eyes looked upon it. The vision of Kingston and that bureau worker she grown to hate flashed in the midst of each scene, physically bringing to life and magnifying the anger, sending it skyrocketing through her entire body!

~ Twenty-Nine ~

“Every shove from ‘that guy’ was intersected with a shove by me. BOOM! Like a missile being dropped in a war zone.

“I remembered feeling like I was dreaming, but I wasn't; I was awake. And something more powerful that I’d ever felt kept tugging and tugging, and I was losing control. I could see, but everything was black and red like lava. All the images I’d been pushing out my head came swooping toward me.

“I remembered an explosion, but it was hazy, as if I wasn’t really there. It wasn’t until recently that I learned the car fire had spread over the garage, across the entire yard, to the backside of the house. Things had gotten out of control. There was a lot of fighting back and forth. I could list the things that have been done to me, but I offer no excuses for my actions because my actions weren’t solutions.

“Now that I can tell my story and be totally open and honest, my rage had nothing to do with my victims. Truthfully, my life had equipped me with more than enough tools to deal with those petty blows. Had I been in a healthy place mentally, he wouldn’t have even been an associate. But I guess my mind no longer had the capacity to hold all the things stuffed inside.”

Taking some time before trusting herself to continue speaking, she begins choking with emotion, feeling herself starting to reduce. At the same time, she is mindful of where her silence has gotten her, so she grips onto the ledge, then whispers, “It’s like everything in my life was happening so quickly I couldn’t stop it and they were happening so slowly I couldn’t see what was1 approaching me.”

Her grip weakened, she is descending and unable to stop. A slow long drop and Zoe knows there’s no parachute or safety net to suspend the fall.

Dr. Brooks leans across her desk, pleading with Zoe. “Please give your body permission to release everything. Don’t hold back any more. I know it hurts, but it’s the only way you’ll move forward.”

Body heaving, slumped slightly over, Zoe weeps as if she’s attending a funeral for herself. A welling cry pours out for all the years stolen, for all the years wasted, for all her wrongdoing, and for all the people rooted in her life, yet she is only able to break the silence with, basically, a total stranger. Many of the tears are for letting down her grandmother and children. Some are because she knows her opponents are squatting and laughing in a corner like critters. She cries for all the new boundaries she will now have to set for herself and for the boundaries she’ll have to set for the people she loves.

Then something strange happens. She realizes not only are her tears for this list of deeds, misdeeds, herself, and all these other people, but there are also tears of joy. There was a whisper within her while she wept that said, “Now, if you’re willing to surrender and do your part, all of your oppositions can be your opportunity.” She feels a crack in her spirit like a lobster cracking out of its shell, and she knows she's just outgrown the capsule she's been trapped in for way too long.

As this joyous feeling finds room in this office filled with heaviness, Zoe looks up into Dr. Brooks' face and sees that maybe her story is different, but they both are clinging to the victory of being survivors of a storm.

"I was my father, my mother, my grandmother; I was other family members too. I was a piece of all my abusers. I was Vinny. I was parts of my friends and associates. I was even a piece of the neighbors from down the street. I was so many things I didn't want to be. Worst of all, I couldn't find me."

They sit there in a few brief moments of quietness. Zoe suddenly feels her heart begin to race and the panic starts rising fast at the thought of her not knowing who she is. Almost everything she's done, almost every place she's gone, almost every emotion she's experienced has been at the steering wheel of someone else's hand.

Her lips begin to tremble as she says, "I lost myself. I don't even know what my hobbies are. It's like my body and my spirit are complete opposites."

To ease the discomfort, she forces herself to produce a little laugh, even though she doesn't think it is remotely funny, but she has to do something to keep from going back in the drowning waters. Then she attempts to give a closet excuse by saying, "I'm always helping other people and sometimes it's hard to say no. Before I know it, I'm being pulled in all sorts of directions."

What a typical explanation, right? Well, that's only a portion of the truth. The other portion of the truth is she's been running from herself, which they both already know. And although Zoe doesn't disclose much of herself to people, there are still some things people know and she's aware of how strong they think she is. There's no question that most days she could have stayed in bed, and there were just as many days she just wanted to give up. Not only was it the outright complimentary words, but it was also the times people came to her for help and those situations when people appeared to be braver with her presence. Those are the reinforcing reasons she knows her greatest enemy isn't other people. Regardless of all the strikes swung by human beings, Zoe now understands she's become her own greatest enemy.

Dr. Brooks bites down on her bottom lip, gently nodding, preparing to speak. "Zoe, you've been carrying an impossible amount of secrecy and agony that has held power over you. All those piercing, broken pieces shattered everywhere, like tiny bombs. At any given time, someone could trigger one, and kaboom, causing you to relive the trauma as if for the first time. A lot of people who have encountered unfortunate events, such as your experiences and like our veterans, who have also endured unspeakable events, are commonly diagnosed with Post Traumatic Stress Syndrome. I am positive you are suffering from PTSD. However, after reviewing the details of your case, and with us working together, I'm confident you can live a happy and safe life.

"You see, it is extremely difficult to talk about something when there are no words to describe it, but you have to find a word, even if it's the wrong word, otherwise you'll remain stuck in the initial shock. And, as you've learned, suppressed memories don't stay suppressed. They keep forcing their way to the surface. The body won't allow those kinds of memories to be pushed aside permanently. Sometimes, there are moments in our lives when we are blindsided, and another consequence of our silence is we can temporarily become a statistic. There is no common knowledge to cope with the strain of trauma.

"Not wanting to accept the toll abuse has played in our lives is also part of the reason why we'd rather not confront the damages because, for many people, their defense mechanism is, 'I ain't nobody's victim.' I want you to see how, throughout your life, every transgression against you, every stand you've taken, every loyalty act you've performed and that was performed in your favor, every exit and entrance, has stitched together another panel in your belief system. The feeling of being lost isn't necessarily a bad thing. From a positive aspect, it could mean your inner being is refusing to settle in an uncomfortable place. When you look at it from that point of view, being lost can be the beginning of transforming and being rebirthed."

~ Thirty ~

Zoe gets out of bed the next morning after her appointment with Dr. Brooks, feeling as if she's been tied in a knot and knocked off a bridge. Every part of her body aches. Her eyes are burning and her lids are heavy. She bends forward, touching her toes, trying to stretch out the tightness, and all her bones crack. She takes a hot shower, standing directly beneath the water as though it can wash away the work she knows she'll have to put forth in order to heal properly. Tenseness clamps down at the fear of no longer having Band-Aids and being exposed to a vulnerability that is now generating much regret. She believes that same vulnerability was the cause of her initial attacks. But it is too late. The journey up to this part has already changed her, leaving no choice except to proceed.

After drying the wetness from her face, she's disturbed by the reflection in the mirror peering back at her. The plushness of her cheeks has shrunk and her skin looks thinly pulled over her bony, sunken face. Parts of her hair are long and other parts are broken off. She is even more startled by the bleakness in her eyes. Zoe has seen herself like this before, but this is the first time she's looked worse than she feels. It is always the other way around.

A faint smile materializes once the realization settles that she is being fixed this time in an organic and spiritual way. She can feel it in her core, and instead, there comes some sense of confidence that when the inside is healed, the outside will be restored. Although, physically. the raw pain still exists, she knows she's becoming stronger, and that's what she chooses to hold on to.

Again, Zoe feels she's out on the edge of a world unknown and there's no way of predicting her future once she dives off the cliff. But she knows she has to jump, so the "cloned her" formed by man can die and the woman God created her to be can live. In the beginning of this process, she's fallen into a novel region without a compass, and she has to be extra careful not to use any of her many self-destructive coping mechanisms because of the discomfort. Dr. Brooks told her "some wounds will never heal, but you can live peacefully with the scars". She consciously dies every single morning she wakes up until the day comes that a new Zoe is born.

❧✹☙

She and Dr. Brooks work on all possible areas before readdressing the topic of Zoe's family. She is afraid of what people will think or say, and she also believes to speak her feelings will be committing an ultimate betrayal against her loved ones.

"Now that you're speaking from a much-healthier place, what are your thoughts and feelings regarding the relationship with your mother?"

She struggles with suppressing the sharpness in her heart, not of jealousy or anger, but from the yearning for an intimate friendship. After taking time before responding, she says, "My mother is a good person by nature. She's sweet, polite, and educated. She works hard to provide for her children, and anything I've ever asked for, she'd always find a way to make it possible. Although I was happy with the gifts and financial support, it was not the presents I needed, it was her presence.

"I thought over the years I had accepted our relationship for what it was, but when those random incorrect comments were made that would begin to hurt, it was a reminder of how little she really knew about me. However, my mother has taught me so many things. If it wasn't for witnessing her strengthen during the aftermath of her silent aching, I wouldn't have been able to rise back up each time I stumbled. And there's no way I could've endured all this without being bitter. She showed me how to lift my head up high and not to be afraid to walk alone down any darkened road, how to put my life back together as smoothly, as sublimely, as gracefully as it can be done, by being positive and putting in overtime, and to never let go of my faith."

"What are your thoughts and feelings regarding the relationship with your father?"

"I don't know if my father's rage developed while he was serving in Vietnam and maybe the war is the cause of him being devoid of other emotions, but then there's the possibility of him just being wired this way."

The thought that he may have just chosen to live without her revives a twinge of grief. She pauses at the thought and is mindful of the feeling. Then she decides to continue moving forward, not allowing it to take root, because she knows she can't reach her destination driving in reverse.

"I think about when I was a young girl, I'd watch my father move like a machine in the most macho way a human being could. After he got off his second shift job at midnight, he'd shovel all the snow before going to bed, and we had a pretty big yard. When we traveled, he'd drive clean across the country without hardly taking a rest. Everything broken or that needed to be repaired, he fixed it with his bare hands. But what stands out most is remembering the proudness he showed after he'd go shopping and fill the kitchen and back hallway with bags and cases of food, and the enjoyment on his face when he'd sit outside all day, helping my mother plant her flowers.

"One of the sweetest, most sincere things I remember is him having long, deep conversations with my grandmother. I always saw him sucking up, craving more of her wisdom. He showed me that being a grown man isn't contingent upon the pounds he can lift, and that it takes more than money for a man to support and be in harmony with his family. Perhaps it is the fact that I have this personal knowledge as evidence that there is a good man somewhere inside my father which gives a soft radiation of solace that won't permit my hurt to form into hatred. My father has also shown me through his absence all the previous memories and moments I will miss if I don't learn to let go and to forgive.

"Now that I've personally learned from my own losses and failed love and reinventions, and I've learned more about my people's history and the history of being born a woman, I can see my mother through a telescope lens, zoomed out, revealing a much wider view other than my narrow view of her as only a mother."

Again, knowledge furnishes understanding; it reveals truth—the truth of a woman, a black woman at that, who's been psychologically assaulted and penalized by every race, including our own men, for being full-figured and having rhythm, with a dark silk, permanent tan. An undeniably irresistible and strong brand, yet forced into being a dirty little secret, and deemed not feminine enough to always be treated as a queen. But, like that old saying goes, "You don't miss a good thing until it's gone."

"My mother rose higher than the mountain of debris, thrusting past the expectation of wives and mothers being domestic workers. She was part of a movement just as critical as Rosa Parks and Dr. King Jr. My mother is part of the generation of black women paving the road for their children to be educated, to be business owners, and for their voices to be heard. Now I understand my father's devastation when my mother said, 'No, you do not get another chance.'

"Just like my mother, I found that life has a way of falling into an eclipse which declines and shadows out all language. And, just like my father, I mastered grand finales. Think about the things I've done: good and bad, the things I wish I could have done differently, the things I wouldn't change, and those things no one else could ever understand. It is only because of my willingness to reflect over my own movements and journey that I was able to grasp sympathy. With knowing, there is always a story behind the story that has gifted me with a more in-depth thought process."

This is the first time Zoe is able to go deeper beneath the surface of unworthiness.

"By the time my twenty-ninth birthday arrived, had I known the symptoms, I would've known at my celebration I was entering the heart of a nervous breakdown. The things I loved and believed in instantly became invaded by a murky fog, leaving an invisible hole exceeding the size of my ability to leap over. Everything seemed like a film of cobwebs floating in the air compared to the pain enveloping my world. When we've been trained to dissociate the pressing sensuous need from the most essential departments of our lives other than intercourse, we begin using sexual mates as a passport to travel through life. I had no idea I was giving their spirits permission to enter my body and how it was affecting me internally.

"One minute I'd have my own motive and I could easily see the difference between the other person and me. Then, a day would come when I would discover I'd flipped on myself, and rather than only entertaining trouble, I too became troubled."

Zoe commences to smiling. It is that same bright, hopeful smile she had as a child before the enemy tried to steal it away. She looks at Dr. Brooks and says, "Did you know I was supposed to be dead? I've got more lives than a cat, and not only did God save me, He preserved me in such a way that I don't even look like all I've been through. Some people think I'm lucky. Some people think my life has had more than its fair share of misery, but I know now that I'm blessed. By being in the presence of and closely observing so many different people, I've learned that human misery only dwells in those who never find the key to be awakened. So, in the grand scheme of everything, I am truly thankful."

~ Thirty-One ~

The process for Zoe's recovery consisted of many diversions of levels throughout her life, which led up to her breakdown. One of the things that became unbearable (other than constantly being haunted by her past) was the fact that subconsciously she thought she had exhausted every step advised by a variety of people to strengthen herself, like exercising, eating organic foods, taking vitamins, having a religion, and reading success books. None of it made her feel whole and human. After breaking down, after the explosion, when there was no more running away from situations or from herself, there were no words. Every thought had vanished and she didn't speak; she cried for months.

Then a whisper came into her ear; maybe it was her guardian angel softly asking every so often, "Are you going to live? Or, are you going to die?"

She hadn't forgotten the promise she'd made to God all those years ago that she would never again attempt to take her own life. And since He'd decided to keep her heart beating, dying wasn't an option, but she didn't know how she could live. When Zoe began talking honestly with Dr. Brooks about her life, a natural healing began to happen at a faster pace than ever before. However, her compass was still deficient. In addition to speaking regularly with the doctor, she worked closely with her spiritual counselor, read the Bible, and meditated.

The reverend continuously shared, "Everything you need is living inside you." It felt so good to hear those words, even though there was a shortage in the connection. She recognized this place; she'd been there before. Then her spirit said loud and clear, "Do not proceed with any speed." Following the orders, she drank infant formula, eventually she crawled, then she took baby steps. She needed help understanding why and how things were happening. Many scriptures in the Bible kept popping out at her, saying, "Seek knowledge."

In the midst of being rebuilt, with a wholehearted desire to be the woman God wanted her to be, a friend sent her a book on the law of attraction. Since the late nineties, she'd heard and come across articles about the law of attraction, and her perception of it up to this point had always been unclear. There was no doubt of it being inspiring, but a part of her felt like it was a rich person's way of humbly explaining their wealth, and there was another part of her that wasn't sure if it was some kind of religion.

In her humility, she had an open mind and began to study the book, prepared to absorb and use whatever was beneficial. It is through the decoding of this teaching that she reached a ground-breaking epiphany. She learned how to identify the non-deliberate vibrations we send out into the universe through the things we observe, allow into our ears, or even by reminiscing, which helped her to constantly check her thought system. She pointed out that lesson because it was one of her biggest hang-ups. She had been told all her life, "You have a choice," or, "It is your responsibility."

She finally learned how to make her spirit overpower her emotions to dominate the influences of her mind. Knowing she attracted the things she gave her attention to helped her to solely focus on the good things instilled in her. Only speaking and pouring her energy into what she wanted to manifest drastically reduced the contrast in all areas of her life, which changed the words she put into the air, which put her in a daily practice of having a positive attitude and actively rotating in a healthy cycle. She aligned herself with every aspect of how she wanted the universe to respond, setting her in a position for God to work in her, through her, and around her.

One day she woke up and realized she was no longer practicing. It had been incorporated into her lifestyle. That was also the day she realized, that along the way, she'd learned the difference between religion and spirituality. For the first time, she not only felt it, but she knew in her spirit she was whole, she was human, and she was living.

Still, of course, there were times when the people she loved poked at some tender spots, and there were also times when those unwanted memories crept around. But she stayed on her path because she knew those feelings were like birds that would quickly fly away. She rejected any sadness by reminding herself that her future was bursting with happiness and blessings. Just below the threshold of consciousness, she'd sometimes fumble, looking for reason people's fickleness, but she had to force herself to also let go of that hidden mishap as well.

Anything that was aroused within herself, she had to hit the reset button to accomplish her goals, to be the mother her children deserved, and for them to inherit God's kingdom on this earth. It demanded she dig into a motherlode of unknown strength; the book of Psalms was what gave her fuel. One of the verses she rested on most was Psalm 46:10, "Be still, and know that I am God."

Zoe began accepting all that had happened were vital pieces to her purpose: the horrors that had haunted her through the night; the spitting volcano that kept appearing with waves of flames cartwheeling toward her; being able to feel the energy from objects; the wicked woman who'd tried to destroy her only because of envy; and the way that huge beautiful tree across the county had drawn her to it and become an organic IV. In those most painful moments, the clouds darkened and poured down rain, but then, in perfect timing, the sun always broke free.

One summery day, her spiritual counselor unexpectedly came into town and showed up at her grandmother's house, which he hadn't visited for years; Zoe just so happened to be there. They'd reconnected just in time for him to teach her and guide her through her largest crisis. She knew all these things were fragments, floating, waiting to be constructed into some sort of sculpture. And every time the image started to become clear, a current would swiftly blow by, causing the picture to become fuzzy again.

Then Zoe understood that this too she had to give up because her eyes were incapable of seeing God's plan. It wasn't as simple as a preview of a single photograph and it was beyond the comparison to a slideshow that you wouldn't understand until the end. All the things she wanted to be or could have been filtered down to an empty sheet. The only option left was for her to be who she was designed to be. She realized she had joined the universal longing for something unrealistic—an ideal human. That was why no person was satisfying; they could only furnish her with a crafty, artistic snapshot.

Through her imagination, she began visualizing and mentally rehearsing her life—minus the shame, anger, bitterness; minus those who refused to work on their inner selves; minus the fears and self-pity and negativity. She created a future by visualizing and pouring something that wasn't imaginary into her vessel, and she could feel her soul saying on this sweet, golden, serene day, "This is how it was meant to be and will always be."

She looked up to the sky and smiled, and felt the affection being returned to her. Most of her life had been spent unlearning how she'd trained herself to cope, how she felt about myself, how to respond to issues, and all the other many problems she needed to get rid of. It was a deeply-abiding faith that provided her with the needed nourishment through those turbulent nights, when her self-worth and dreams vanished, when she had nobody to grab hold to and she had to go through the healing process with no one by her side. Somehow she knew it was ordained that she travel this path alone. Nothing about it was easy. She felt lonelier and more-abandoned than anyone could imagine.

However, it turned out to be another lesson for her to get down into her gut. She reached a place where she knew no one or nothing from the past, or anyone or anything in the future, would hold her captive or destroy any piece of her again. Then she became thankful for the things she had by having been set aside, and for the majority of her family and friends to have lived as if she'd died: A calm heart and the elimination of extorted thinking. Being mindful, not allowing interference. Having awareness of every inch of herself. Sitting in the driver's seat, oblivious to all decoys. Resolving whatever arises before it sinks through the flesh. Obtaining enlightenment, satisfaction, and peace regardless of surroundings. Existence during such moments is the greatest miracle and an uncanny reality. Like a baby bird living a small portion of its life blinded, you watch the film fade from the third eye—your spiritual eye—and your vision becomes as clear as a curious child's. A found freedom to fully live each minute of life. That miracle is equivalent to the sea understanding its boundaries.

Zoe had to understand and identify her weaknesses and remove herself from that, then set lines in place to keep certain things away from her. The things that use to matter didn't matter anymore. Everything became about her only wanting to coddle and nourish her inner being. She used to think fancy clothes hugging her waistline just right were what made her look so sexy. She thought her MAC lips and virgin hair were her best accessories. She used to look at sex as a way to keep a man's inner demands at bay. Then she viewed it as emotions unleashed in the dark, not wanting to be recognized in the light of day. For the females she'd encountered in society, copulation was stimulation enough.

Now a relationship is formed within herself, and when she falls in love with this woman, it is only then that she's capable of totally connecting with her spirit, and that's when she finds the landscape and is able to read the blueprint leading into her heart.

☙❁❧

To what degree of this inward journey Dr. Brooks detects within her, Zoe isn't sure. During their sessions, they speak mostly about the past and different ways of managing anxiety. Some people say the awful things in life happen by wickedness or by accident, but do those people forget that the prophecy has to be fulfilled? Zoe almost did. As Zoe walks to the soft melody of her own tones, readying herself to constitute everything that has occurred into the rhythm of her steps, she sits down and writes in her journal as dawn oozes over the sky:

Yesterday almost killed you, but through the night you were reborn, and today you will live.

She has to consciously decide to allow herself to become a student again. While dealing with her own highs and lows, her actions, her hidden pain, her spirit, she has learned to identify with and understand other people's struggles. While attending to her own, she is blessed with a prescription of forgiveness. There comes a time when our lives are divided into two separate parts: the time before, which seems so far away it's hard to fathom, and the time afterward, which is so prestigious and profound, it's the only thing you can see. She moves slowly across the plush green field, almost feeling as though she's gliding.

No longer weighed down by the chains of death as she passes by the trees, they sway as if they are rejoicing. Through the brushes is a narrow passage, then the ground begins lowering like grass has grown over the stairs. At the bottom lies a bed of sand framing the blue lake. She stands there, staring out at the water, beneath the warmth of the sun, and she understands—like the survivors of a hurricane when the tropical cyclone of winds has finally ceased and the pavement has been restored to dry land. Collapsing onto her knees and falling forward onto her hands, tears of thankfulness and joy stream down, forming puddles of mud. Praying and worshiping alongside the waves of the obedient waters, all her fears and pains are washed away. Her flesh is calm and there's a great comfort in her body, and in her head, there is nothing but clarity.

Doctor Brooks looks directly into her eyes and says, "Ms. Zoe Stone," with a smile of approval, "I want you to speak from your heart and into the heart of someone who is in desperate need of inspiration."

Zoe pauses and considers her words before speaking. She thinks, *'What could someone have said to me that could have possibly make any difference?'*

Without overthinking it, she passionately speaks exactly what she's feeling. "Everyone won't understand my journey. I realize how strangely I was sculpted by the many storms, the many teachers, my ancestors, and my many blessings. It required a whole lot of staples to hold all that's in me together, but now I can hold my head up high in a room filled with dignitaries, spine straight, chest lifted, shoulder blades tapping, like a proud lioness, interlaced with emblems, with grooves, with a strong set of beliefs, a small amount influenced by villains, but mostly by the guidance of divine order. How powerfully all that happened has shaped my life.

"Ever since I can remember, I hid behind a veil of concealed problems that essentially necessitated so much mental and emotional energy to maintain. But no longer afraid, I want to encourage victims or family members of victims to tell someone, "I NEED HELP!"; for others to see the truth beneath the surface of their pain and to embrace self-correction, even if you are the parent. There's an obligation to notice certain signs that your child may be in some kind of danger.

"And more than anything, please don't ignore that burning desire to tell anyone who will listen, 'There is nothing God can't bring you through or heal you from, then use you for the glory of His grace,' because you don't know how those words will help someone get through their day."

☙❁❧

Those are all the things which inspired the writing of my ministry. I was afraid of everything, and I ran from everything until I realized, "You can't find yourself running." I have never really tested myself against myself. Through it all, my prayers and the prayers sent from my loved ones sustained me, and in the end, prayer delivered me.

I believe He revealed my experiences to show who He is, "The Epitome of Love."

Signed by: The Spirit That Can't Be Broken

As I wrote, giving snippets of the various divisions of my life—silently suffering issues too painful to speak aloud; too afraid the painful words would cause an indescribable discomfort to my loved ones; spending my life up to this point hiding every injury, every unpleasant or offensive thing—I had to resist the usage of enticing words. I had to disavow myself of those hiding places I'd become accustomed to, those hiding places easily found when writing. Using symbolic or metaphoric terminology couldn't convey the entire story behind the story because, for me, being fondled, raped, beaten, abandoned, sold, seeing flesh fighting to hold on to its soul, did not resemble "a rough patch", nor did it feel like "the calm before the storm", nor was it anything like "a peaceful fallen dove".

I'd tried every way I knew to set my mind free. It makes me wonder how many kids could be saved if they were led to the proper outlet for their emotions, instead of drowning in them. This is a declaration of freedom and wisdom of what is needed: love, confidence and spirituality. As a child, life showed me I wasn't exempt from the possibility of injury and that nothing is guaranteed, not even protection. As a young adult, I figured out that sex, parties, religion, and being a hard worker with all the motivation and passion weren't enough to hold back all the shadows from my past.

Upon seeking healing and knowledge, I found myself; then peace and joy anchored my feet solidly to the ground. I did not get to those places on my own and I did not get to this place on my own either. Now, as a full-flowered, rooted woman, that still voice kept His promise: my oppositions did transform into my opportunities.

~ Epilogue ~
Food for Thought

Trauma and abuse are broadcast publicly through the homes and streets of our country—the history of oppression; the shame and confusion branded in the faces of our children, distorting their inner beings, continuing to swing the same whips used to destroy and brainwash our ancestors.

Whether you're inflicting pain, or you're the one ignoring the warning signs, or you're the one who discounts it as minor, you are actively keeping the legacy of slavery alive. The grim lashes from being degraded, raped, robbed, left unprotected, and violated are molding and defining the futures for our youth.

Resources

National Human Trafficking Resource Center
1-888-373-7888

City of Milwaukee Office of Violence Prevention
1-414-286-3521

National Domestic Violence Hotline call 24 hours
1-800-799-7233

National Hotline for Crime Victims
1-855-4-VICTIM (1-855-484-2846)

National Stalking Resource Center
1-202-467-8700

National Suicide Prevention Lifeline
1-800-273-TALK (8255) [24/7 hotline]
1-888-628-9454 (Spanish)
1-800-799-4889 (TTY)

The Trevor Project – Crisis & Suicide Prevention Lifeline for LGBTQ Youth
1-866-488-7386

National Sexual Assault Hotline
1-800-656-4673

Identity Theft Resource Center
1-888-400-5530

National Alliance on Mental Illness
1-800-950-6264

National Association of Crime Victim Compensation Boards
1-703-780-3200

National Child Abuse Hotline
1-800-422-4453

National Advocacy for Local LGBT Communities
1-212-714-1141

National Indigenous Women's Resource Center
1-406-477-3896

National Runaway Switchboard
1-800-786-2929

National Sexual Assault Hotline
1-800-656-4673 [24/7 hotline]

National Teen Dating Abuse Helpline
1-866-331-9474 or 1-866-331-8453 (TTY)

Parents of Murdered Children
1-888-818-7662

National Women's Law Center
1-202-588-5180